WITHIN THE BIBLE

Presented To:

Name			
From			
Date		Time	
Location			
Occasion			
Signed			

Written By Mr. Mandinko Dee
Edited By MA.EN Publishing Services
Email: info@maenkingdom.com

Table of Contents

Introduction

My earthly father, although a devout Christian like many others who were farmers, used a yellow book called the Mac Donald's Almanac which depicted specific time frames by which to plant in alignment with the planets in order for crops to grow bigger.

At the back of that book there were some extremely supernatural subjects that my father and other Christian farmers would completely ignore; as if they knew what to sift out as per what was relevant. I realized after that farming by the almanac was astrology in its fullest sense and that there was a certain negative stereotypical perspective toward astrology in particular from Christians that had to be addressed, although they conveniently overlooked certain parts of it.

I've witnessed how little the crops would grow when they weren't planted in alignment with the moon in contrast to how large they would when they were. I've noticed how accurate elderly women's assessments were in determining when a child would be born as per alignment with the moon, nullifying the estimated dates of medical doctors.

Fishermen know when to catch turtles laying eggs on the beach as per alignment. Many hairstylists have the wisdom of cutting hair in the alignment for longer, thicker and fuller hair. The three biblical wise men were able to astrologically distinguish a star in the east to confirm the birth time and location of The Christ.

Practical life as well as biblical illustrations are revealed in this magnificent book as we accept our admonishment to prove all things and hold fast to what is true. May this book provide the enlightenment and balance needed in order for many to acquire more grounding in their application of the appropriate astrological factors into their lives.

The Author

Acknowledgements

YHWH: The first and highest level of acknowledgment, gratitude and ultimate source of my inspiration goes to my number 1 ; Who has always been and will ever be, the greatest influence on my person: My Grand Master; Healer, Provider, Protector and Source of my consciousness: My Divine Father Who has provided me with the wisdom, knowledge and understanding for me to be......and therefore I am..... By the powers of the Great "I AM" .

Sir Josser Vannecko: My late, great earthly father and hero, who taught me that common sense and inspiration are the parents of education. The one who was able to provide me with answers as a child that the most educated religious leaders still can't decipher up to date .

Mrs. Mandinko Dee: The triple cardinal Queen; by date, day and numerology (master number 11)....as well as and the most beautiful person inside and out; the wind beneath my wings .

Jenifer Bernice: My older sibling who took care of me as my first mom, then grew to become my best friend, establishing an unbreakable bond; You've always been in my corner as I'll always be in yours.

To my mom, Marian Elenita: You taught me how to be consistent in faith. You never panicked in a crisis because your exemplary faith was real and powerful; it prolonged the life of your husband and saved the life of your eldest son.

To my sons and daughter: Arthur, Nathaniel, Sharif & Julie Dee: Born winners; my pride and joys. Just as you arise after each battle that you face, will you stand victorious after the war.

Allison Williams: Tribute to an amazing person and one of the Caribbean's greatest bodybuilding and fitness athletes, who competed and won locally and placed internationally. After our many deep discussions, you were the first to ever insist that I begin to write and the first motivation to do so.

BOOKS PUBLISHED

#	Name	Published	Launched
1.	Spirit of Lion, Dragon & Dove	Wed Nov 25 '20	Sat Dec 19 '20
2.	**Astrology Within The Bible**	**Sat Mar 30 '24**	**Sat Mar 30 '24**

ASTROLOGY
WITHIN THE BIBLE

Mandinko Dee

Chapter 1:
The Difference Between Astronomy & Astrology

1. As per dictionary: Astronomy is the study of the universe and its contents above the earth. Astronomers examine the positions, motions, and properties of celestial objects. Astrology attempts to study how those positions, motions and properties affect people and events on earth.
2. Some people often go to the section in the newspapers to discover what their horoscope says with regards to what their day, year or lives will be like, according to their zodiac signs. Others may view astrology as an evil or demonic ritual that everyone should stay away from. I've even been told that the studying of one's zodiac is idol worship.
3. Although some Christians would state that both astronomy and astrology are both demonic, some Christians would say that astronomy is alright and that it's "astrology" that is bad. When I read the explanation of both as per verse "1", I must admit that astronomy seems to be a summary of astrology and therefore remains concealed. Astronomy conceals the extent of Astrology in it's summary thereof.
4. The astronomical studying of the universe and its contents above or outside doesn't ascertain as to what level one is studying and could also entail the affects of the motions on life as well, as is depicted to define astrology. On the other hand studying the effects of the positions, motions and properties of the elements do not necessarily need to be crossing any definitive boundaries of astrology either.
5. Based on the fact that astronomy and astrology seem to mean the same thing, whereas astronomy is the generalization of astrology and can be found in practical life as well as can be supported biblically, I think it's appropriate to hereby concur that we can cover everything under the singular topic of astrology in the stead of speculating between the two.

Chapter 1:
The Difference Between Astronomy & Astrology

6. The summary of any story can be better explained in the detailed manner. It is for this reason, to be more precise or to give more clarity, we delve into the detailed version of the topic. A good comparison of the difference between astronomy and astrology would be religion and Christianity. Whilst religion covers all the variety of beliefs, Christianity only covers 1 minor section within religion.
7. It would therefore be meaningless to use Christianity to cover the meaning of religion. Christianity would not suffice to convey a message of what religion is whereas its capacity is not large enough to do so. One would therefore do much better to go into the concepts that explain what religion is and how it was established. E.g. if we were to explain that religion was established as a means for political control, it's comprehension would climb to another level.
8. Now if the objective is to study Christianity, religion would not suffice either. Religion would not cover the specifics of Christianity, as there are so many religions with different concepts and beliefs: Studying Christianity under the topic of religion would then be the correct comparison.
9. Compared to astrology; if we are to explain that astrology was established by God in order to establish a structure whereby humans can know their particular role in life, the world would have a more organized manner of functioning. It's now understandable why astrology is like Christianity and astronomy religion (more generalized).
10. Astro means relating to the stars or celestial objects or outer space whilst nomy means "donating a specified area of knowledge or the laws governing it.
11."Astro" is the beginning part of astrology.
Logy means dull and heavy in motion or thought, or sluggish. The term astro at the beginning of astronomy as well as astrology both mean pertaining to the planets and celestial bodies !

Chapter 2:
Clarification of Astrology in the Bible

1. Astrology, which is defined by it's attempt to study how the positions, motions and properties of the planets affect people and events on earth should not be judged to be sorcery or witch craft. As per Bible the earth is indeed stagnant; whilst actually its the sun, moon and other planets (also called stars) that move; their movements determine the quantity of light by day and by night; That in itself confirms the acknowledgment of astrology.
2. The following bible texts seem to imply the earth's stagnation. Psalm 104:5 He established the earth upon its foundations, So that it will not be removed forever and ever. 1 Chronicles 16:30 Tremble before Him, all the earth; Indeed, the world is firmly established, it will not be moved. Psalm 93:1 The LORD reigns, He is clothed with majesty; The LORD has clothed and girded Himself with strength; Indeed, the world is firmly established, it will not be moved.
3. As per Genesis 1:14 All the planets are called lights. Their purpose is to divide the day from the night, for signs, seasons and days as well as to determine the years. Genesis 1 verse 16 further goes on to explain that there were two great lights that stood out; The greater one (the sun) was to rule the day and then a lesser one to rule the night (the moon). The rest of the planets were referred to as stars.
4. Whilst all the other planets seem to have their purpose, its as if bible is saying that the Sun and moon are the two most relevant or significant of the planets.
It's imperative that we at least come to an agreement with the terms of planets, stars and worlds. In order for me to come to a mutual place of agreement with you the reader, I hereby propose to refer to all as planets, but differentiate that a world is a planet that accommodates life force that the other planets were designed to accommodate.

Chapter 2:
Clarification of Astrology in the Bible

5. I will further state that it is my present conviction that the planets are meant to accommodate our world; designed to accommodate our lives on planet earth. The reason why I state "my present conviction" is because I always keep an open mind to learn new things as I'm also of the realization that we don't know everything. It's important to ever be prepared to discard what we know in order to accept a better concept derived from the acquisition of the understanding of more knowledge.

6. I also do believe that there are other worlds out there that have their own sun, moon and stars to accommodate their worlds. This biblical clarification of Genesis chapter 1 verse 14, seems to be referring to the planets that accommodate "our" world, as "lights"; the greater light to rule the day seems to be the sun, whereas the lesser light to rule the night seems to be the moon.

7. In verse 16 of Genesis chapter 1 whereby it is stated that He made the stars also, seems to be a compilation of all the other planets besides the sun and moon which may imply to mean, Mars, Mercury, Jupiter, Venus, Saturn, Neptune and Uranus. If we were to list all of the planets that accommodate our world; planet earth, it may not be in the sequence mentioned above. The sequence will fall in alignment with the sequence of which planet matches which day as stipulated in verse 8 below

8. 1st The Sun, 2nd The Moon, 3rd Mars, 4th Mercury, 5th Jupiter, 6th Venus, 7th Saturn ….. the 8th and 9th would be Neptune and Uranus.

Bible gives clarification in Psalms 104:19 that the moon is the determining factor for the seasons whereas the statement of the sun knowing it's going down, implies not only that the sun is the determining factor for the days, but also has a fixed pattern. As the sun rises up and goes down: Its going down "ends" each day whereas its rising "starts" the day (Genesis 1:16).

Chapter 2:
Clarification of Astrology in the Bible

9. Further clarification of astrology in the bible, can be found in Mathew 2:2 where the three wise men knew when and where the baby Christ was born due to reading the stars and seeing His star in the east.
Other astrological signs of the planets were the moon turning red and the sun becoming dark. Those predictions are found in Joel 2:31, Acts 2:20, Mathew 24:29 and Revelation 6:12. Mathew 24:29 even goes further to predict a meteoric shower.
10. In may 19th of the year 1780 was the first time noted that the moon turned into blood (meaning red) and the sun simultaneously went dark, which was known as the dark day. As per the bible texts provided above, it is impossible not to see that these events did indeed happen as was predicted.
Mathew 24:25's statement of the stars falling from the sky is in reference to meteoric showers
11. During August of 1584, it was said we had the first meteoric shower. In essence bible is using signs of the zodiac to depict the closeness of his second coming; that is a "sign". So planets are obviously being used for signs, contrary to what is professed by some people and astrology is in fact "in" the bible and is the determining factor for signs, days, weeks, months and years. May we therefore hereby concur that astrology "is" in the bible.
12. It is with absolute clarity that Genesis 1:16 is clearly saying that the sun determines the day and that the moon determines the night. We reminisce that as per the primary part of Psalms 104:19, bible confirms that it's the moon that determines the seasons, which are in sequence: Spring, Summer, Autumn and Winter. At this point it would be difficult for anyone not to see that astrology is not only found in the Bible but is also the foundation for signs and times for the functioning of the world we live in.

Chapter 3:
Signs, Days, Months & Years determined by planets

1. Signs are the first thing mentioned in Genesis 1:14. Signs vary from the display of different appearances of planets to time of births, which determine c
2. 36ore characters. We must not evade the meaning of signs or a sign. It is inevitable not to acknowledge that signs are signs; zodiac signs are signs that distinguish our core characters and basic talents. It gives a head start as to how to work with our children as well as what to expect from certain employees based on their time of birth.

2. As per the dictionary, let us look at what a sign means or what signs displayed in a plural form means: a sign can be depicted as traffic sign to give "direction". A sign can also be called a hint. A sign is not a prediction by any means. Whenever astrology leads to prediction or predictions, it is going beyond the intention of a sign. A sign gives guidance. I never read predictions for the day, in newspaper adds, nor do I join any groups that lead to fortune telling, based on astrology, because that is not the purpose of a sign.

3. When we notice a child likes to sing; that may be a "sign" that the child may grow up to be a singer. When a child is good in math , that child may grow up to become an accountant. If a child is physically inclined, that may grow up to be an athlete. A traffic sign gives "direction" (not a prediction) where to go. As per genesis 1:14, signs linked to planets are for navigational directions (e.g. North Star), biblical predictions and zodiac "signs.

4. Note that the sequence after signs are seasons, days and years; without adding or taking away. A sign is not a prediction; neither are zodiac signs. Genesis 1:16 states that He made the greater light (The Sun) to rule the day and the lesser light (The moon) to rule the night. Although the sunlight and moonlight distinguishes the day time from the night time, the planets also play a role in distinguish-

Chapter 3:
Signs, Days, Months & Years determined by planets

5. In addition to just daytime, the sun also determines which day of the week it also is. As per Joshua 10:13 and Psalms 19:4-6, the sun seems to be in a chamber that circles overhead the earth with an obvious slight shift to the south during the ending part of the year and an obvious slight shift to the north during the earlier part of the year as the earth stands still (Psalms 104:5)
6. It seems as if although the sun is the governing planet for daylight, the actual day it is, is based on the alignment with it's planet. The moon, the second greatest light seems to be the second day of the week and the other main planets seem to govern the remaining days of the week. The alignment of the sun with the other planets seem to distinguish each day in a particular manner.
7. The 1st day of the week, "Sunday" (Sun's day), is determined by the sun itself, the greatest light.
The 2nd day of the week, Monday (Moon's day), is named after the 2nd greatest light.
The 3rd day of the week, Tuesday (Mar's day..Martes in Spanish), is named after the planet Mars.
The 4th day of the week, "Wednesday" (the high day) seems to be named after Mercury (Miercules in Spanish)
8. The 5th day of the week, "Thursday" seems to be named after the planet Jupiter (Jueves in Spanish)
The 6th day of the week, "Friday" (Viernes in Spanish) seems to be named after the planet Venus
The 7th day of the week "Saturday" seems to be named after the planet Saturn (Sabado in Spanish means Sabbath).
9. As per astrology "again", each day was created and has a particular alignment from the sun with the planet that determines which day it is. Sunday seems to stand alone whereas the other planets alignment with the sun determines what day it is.

Chapter 3:
Signs, Days, Months & Years determined by planets

... An honorable scientist should be able to wake up from a coma, take a telescope and determine which day of the week it is based on the alignment of the planets

10. As for the determination of the months; I've heard theories which state that a human year is the compilation of the 9 months we carry our babies whereas babies remain in the mother's womb for 9 months. These theorists focus on the time frame every species carries their fetuses in their wombs to determines the equivalence of "their" year. Because of the structure of astrology, I personally am not in accordance.

11. Although the typical year as we know it seems to commence on January 1st, I pay attention to the fact that the 12 zodiac signs fall in alignment with some citizens of India, whose new year begins on March 22nd and falls just a difference of 1 day to Aries, the 1st sign of the zodiac, followed by Taurus the 2nd, Gemini the 3rd, Cancer the 4th, Leo the 5th, Virgo the 6th, Libra the 7th, Scorpio the 8th, Sagittarius the 9th, Capricorn the 10th, Aquarius the 11th and Pisces the 12th .

12. If we were to align the months with the zodiac they would fall into the sequence that is applied in other nations:

Month 1 Aries would be: Mar 21 to Apr 19
Month 2 Taurus would be: Apr 20 to May 20
Month 3 Gemini would be: May 21 to Jun 20
Month 4 Cancer would be: Jun 21 to Jul 22
Month 5 Leo would be: Jul 23 to Aug 22
Month 6 Virgo would be: Aug 23 to Sep 22
Month 7 Libra would be: Sep 23 to Oct 22

13. As we continue to verse 13:

Month 8 Scorpio would be: Oct 23 to Nov 21
Month 9 Sagittarius would be: Nov 22 to Dec 21
Month 10 Capricorn would be: Dec 22 to Jan 19
Month 11 Aquarius would be: Jan 20 to Feb 18

Chapter 3:
Signs, Days, Months & Years determined by planets

... Month 12 Pisces would be: Feb 19 to Mar 20
Just as there are 12 months to a year, there are 12 disciples, 12 gates to the city and if we're precise with a compass we'll find 12 directions should we apply Revelation 10:13

14. The 12 moon cycles that determines the 12 months to compile a year seems to be quite on target from a biblical perspective. The word month comes from the word moon, in the Spanish language the word moon is literally translated as "Luna" which literally means moon in English. The word month also means moon whereas Monday simply means moon's day. Isn't it on point that the first day of the week is Sunday whereas its interpretation is Sun's day which is in fact the first day of the week and the greater light? Is it also any surprise that the second day of the week is called Monday, which means moon's day and the second greatest light ? (genesis 1:16)

15. Is it possible that the 3rd planet created was Mars for Tuesday, Mercury the 4th for Wednesday, Jupiter the 5th for Thursday, Venus the 6th for Friday and Saturn the 7th for Saturday? Interesting how Saturn is also the 6th planet away from the sun. This will imply that it's the 7th planet in a row, which matches with the 7th day. Saturn which represents Saturday the 7th day, is also the only planet that is surrounded by rings of lights. Could this be a sign ? A "zodiac" sign ?

16. Can we concur that a month means a moon's cycle and that 12 moon cycles (months) determine a year? I think its now quite clear as to how Genesis 1:14 is clarifying that the planets determine the days, weeks, months and years. Week is added in whereas the cycle of 7 days compile a week just as 12 months compile the year. Astrology actually enhances and clarifies the structure in which the handy works of The Almighty is structured together to function effortlessly.

Chapter 3:
Signs, Days, Months & Years determined by planets

17. There's a detailed breakdown that enables us to comprehend how precise and structured the astrological perspective of The Grand Master's design is.

- Sunlight determines the daytime of a day
- Moonlight determines the nighttime of a day

I. Sun's alignment with itself determines Sunday
II. Sun's alignment with the moon determines Monday
III. Sun's alignment with Mars determines Tuesday
IV. Sun's alignment with Mercury determines Wednesday
V. Sun's alignment with Jupiter determines Thursday
VI. Sun's alignment with Venus determines Friday
VII. Sun's alignment with Saturn determines Saturday

- Those 7 days listed above completes a week
- A series of close to 4 weeks determines a month
- A series of up to 12 cycles of the moon (months) determine a year.

18. All watches and clocks have obtained the credibility of time by way of the sun dial. We humans have attempted to decide to turn over a day by using midnight on our watches to determine the beginning of a new day. Biblically however, a new day is deemed from sunset to sunset. As per Genesis 1:5 e.g., the evening "and" the morning comprises a day. Evening represents the "entire" night time whereas morning represents the "entire" daytime. When translated appropriately, Bible is saying that an entire day is comprised of the entire night time and the entire day time.

19. This means that from the moment the sun sets, rises and then sets again is when a day is completed. Sabbath keepers e.g. keep Sabbaths from sunset on Friday until the sun sets again on Saturday Afternoon. Although Christmas is celebrated on December 25th, from the moment the sun sets on the afternoon of the 24th, it is called Christmas "eve", which means Christmas "evening" or the evening of Christmas.

Chapter 3:
Signs, Days, Months & Years determined by planets

20. In all fairness, we need to conclude that the duration of a day is from sunset to sunset and not from 12 am midnight. It is because of the fact that some days are longer than some that we need to have a leap year every 4 years in order for the time to be accurate with the sun dial.
In other cultures where there were 10 months adding up to 360 days per year, a month would be added every 4 years in order to add up to the 365 1/4 days for the year: This was equivalent to adding 1 day to a 365 day cycle every 4 years. If we look at the names of our months, we can clearly see that the names do not match their meanings as per which month of the year it is.
21. There are 2 ways in which their meanings can match up, but first lets look at the names and their meanings: January is listed as our 1st month, February as our 2nd, March 3rd, April 4th (April means to open, which implies it should be the 1st month of the year in actuality), May 5th, June 6th, July 7th, August 8th, September is the 9th month of the year although September comes from the word Septimo which means 7th and therefore should be the 7th month of the year. Also note that September, represented by Libra is the only sign that is not symbolized by animal nor person.
22. October although the 10th month actually comes from Octo which means 8 in Latin and should in reality be the 8th month of the year. November the 11th month of the year comes from the word novem which means 9 in Latin and should be the 9th month of the year. December which is the 12th month of the year comes from the Latin word Decem, which means 10 and should be the 10th month of the year. The A letter is the first letter of the alphabet (April means 1 or origin) whereas if April is listed as the 1st month of the year September would be 7th, October 8th, November 9th and December 10th to match the meaning of their names (See verse 12 of this chapter).

Chapter 4:
The Extremities of Astrology

1. Just like anything else; too much of anything is also bad for us. Although Astrology is a blessing that provides a sense of structure to our lives, there are certain elements that have been incorporated that was not the original intent, and is often used as a means to deter us. Anything that pertains to predicting directly to your day, life, death or future is not the appropriate intent whereas a sign is a direction, not a prediction. The mind is so powerful that if it is put to believe anything, whether good or bad, it can make it come to pass.
2. Some of the things that can cause us to believe and predetermine our lives with our minds are the likes of articles in the newspaper that dare to predict what your day will be like, reading of the palm of your hands to determine your life span, marital or future success or the quality of life you're destined to have are all extremities that are not of the intent of astrology. This often first lures you in with good news until they reach the point of negative predictions.
3. It is very important to stay away from the likes of all of those things that seem to go into an immediate futuristic prediction of your life. Bible does have lots of futuristic predictions based on the general durability of the world in its present state. But never will it go into any direct prediction regarding one's personal life. It is imperative to know that your life is in yours and God's hands and the outcome thereof is based on the choices you make.
4. We all have different roles to fulfill in this life and we therefore have a series of different gifts and talents. Gifts are spiritual and talents are allotted based on our time of birth; we are therefore endowed with spiritual gifts and earthly talents. Our spiritual gifts are usually supernatural abilities divinely granted in order to fulfill our spiritual destiny on earth whilst our earthly talents are our abilities that lead us into a particular path/career.

Chapter 4: The Extremities of Astrology

5. No one was born randomly, everyone has a purpose and role to fulfill with their lives. The way our roles and purposes are decided are based on the time, day and date we were born. Galatians 4:4-6 is implying that Yeshuah birth was scheduled at a particular date in order to endow him with the type of strengths He would need in order to fulfill his mission or purpose on earth. No one should therefore ever be allowed to predetermine our lives, death, future or quality of our lives.
6. On the flip side, astrology is the most prominent means to discover the capacity of the role you were designed to execute or fulfill in this life. It is a guide (sign), not a means of predictive information for fortune telling. The means of utilizing your date of birth to confirm the basis of your role, by discovering your gifts and talents, will be revealed to you in the latter part of the chapters of this wonderful book, mainly in areas such as chapters 5 thru 9.
7. 1 Cor 13:8 so adequately confirms that God means love and that once you're with and in God, no negative predictions regarding your life shall come to pass. What ever anyone thinks or predicts to know will happen or continue to happen to will not come to pass, but will vanish as if it never existed as God/love covers all things and has complete control over all circumstances. Anything can be prayed away or redirected at any given time. Remember however not to read nor follow up on the likes of predictions and fortune telling whereas it prompts our minds to make it happen.
8. It's amazing how the world has been structured via the zodiacs to fit the gifts of everyone into the great puzzle of life in a very intelligently organized way. Know yourself and the fullness of your time and be the best version of yourself that you were born to be, whether a cardinal, fixed or mutable individual.
Go out and make the difference you were born to make !

Chapter 4:
The Extremities of Astrology

9. It is of our opinion that it's important to stay away from indulging in the items listed below and remain focused on what is Godly and Biblically substantiated; and most of all, do not confuse the two nor generalize them.

- Horoscopes
- Quija Boards
- Charlie Charlie
- Soothe Sayers
- Fortune Tellers
- Witches or Wizards

Chapter 5:
The 12 Zodiacs & 4 elements Explained

1. Interestingly just as there were 12 disciples, 12 gates to the city and12 months in a year, there are also 12 zodiac signs. These 12 zodiac signs seem to guide us as to what the sequence of the months should be as well as what element and zodiac sign everyone falls under.
2. As listed in chapter 3 verse 12 (page 8): the 12 zodiacs are listed with Aries as the first month and the last month as Pisces .

I. Months	**II. Dates**	**III. Element**
1 Aries	**Mar 21-Apr 19**	*Fire*
2 Taurus	Apr 20-May 20	*Earth*
3 Gemini	May 21-Jun 20	*Air*
4 Cancer	**Jun 21-Jul 22**	*Water*
5 Leo	Jul 23-Aug 22	*Fire*
6 Virgo	Aug 23-Sep 22	*Earth*
7 Libra	**Sep 23-Oct 22**	*Air*
8 Scorpio	Oct 23-Nov 21	*Water*
9 Sagittarius	Nov 22-Dec 21	*Fire*
10 Capricorn	**Dec 22-Jan 19**	*Earth*
11 Aquarius	Jan 20-Feb 18	*Air*
12 Pisces	Feb 19-Mar 20	*Water*

3. As per the chart listed above the 12 zodiacs are grouped in a variety of 3 columns;
Column 1: The twelve zodiacs of the astrological signs
Column 2: The dates of the 12 zodiacs
Column 3: The four Elements of the 12 zodiacs divided into groups of threes (three zodiacs for per element).

Chapter 5:
The 12 Zodiacs & 4 elements Explained

4. As per the chart on page 15 the 12 zodiacs are also divided into 4 elements:
1. Capricorn, Taurus and Virgo are all Earth Signs.
2. Aries, Leo and Sagittarius are all Fire Signs.
3. Cancer, Scorpio and Pisces are all Water Signs.
4. Libra, Aquarius and Gemini are all Air Signs.
The sequence these elements were placed into holds some very deep relevance.
5. Earth signs are symbolized by earth as well as food, whereas food is derived from earth. It is estimated that humans can survive up until 70 days without food.
Water Signs are symbolized by water: a person may only last up to 7 days without water.
Fire signs are symbolized by light or energy aka life force, chi or pratna. In ancient days a torch of fire was the only means of light. Today its origin is from the same source of energy providing light. The life force can be leaving the body for an estimated time of up to 3 days whilst different parts of the body like the legs or arms may be shutting down before the person dies.
Air Signs are symbolized by air or oxygen; the average human being cannot survive past 7 minutes without air.
6. Now lets do the math:
1st The air signs are most vital; with a 7 minute deadline.
2nd The fire sign (Life Force) with a 3 day dead line.
3rd The water sign with a 7 day deadline.
4th The Earth sign (Food) with a 70 day deadline.
7. Review the Biblical comparison of the elements below.
a. Gen 2:7 depicts Jesus as the **Breath of Life** (Air).
b. Jhn 8:12 depicts Jesus as the **light of the world** (Fire).
c. Jhn 4: 10-14 depicts Jesus as the **water of life** (water).
d. John 6:35 depicts Jesus as the **bread of life** (Food)
Bare in mind that bread is the General Biblical terminology for food. Because food comes from the earth; food therefore represent the earth signs.

Chapter 5:
The 12 Zodiacs & 4 elements Explained

.... It is imperative to note that the very same elements of the zodiacs are the means of reliance Bible uses to portray our reliance on the divine: Food, Water, Fire and Air
8. Let's now look at the visibility of the above mentioned elements:
Food which is most visual and can be easily touched and seen is the least essential to the sustainability of our lives.
Water which can hardly be seen; at times when in a glass, one would have to shake it in order to notice its presence; is more important than food.
Fire which represents light or energy, is less visual than food and water, yet is more essential than both for life.
Air which is literally not seen, is amazingly more essential to life than all the above !
9. Although all elements are for our sustainability, those that are less visual are literally more essential to life than those that aren't. As per Genesis 2:7 it is confirmed that the air we breath is ultimately derived from God. Our breathing in and out which seems effortlessly is actually a 10% of the Holy Spirit that we need in order to exhibit life. In the upper room when Yeshuah wanted to give His disciples more power, he literally breathed the Holy Spirit upon them (John 20: 21-23) in order to give them more power.
10. This course of action seems so similar to Genesis 2:7 where the breathing of His breath into the body formed of dust, brought the body to life and caused it to became a living being/soul. In the upper room breathing upon them gave the disciples more power. May we never underestimate the power of Air along with the other elements of the zodiac for our sustainability. May we also see and acknowledge the relevance of the elements: We can now hereby concur that the Air Element, Water Element, Fire Element and Earth Element of the zodiac are the very same concepts that are found within the Bible.

Chapter 5:
The 12 Zodiacs & 4 elements Explained

11. It is amazing how organized the zodiacs and the elements of the zodiacs are. Every element generalizes three zodiac signs that fall under Air, Water, Fire and Earth elements. The Holy City (aka The New Jerusalem) has the very same structure as the zodiac's alignments with their elements.

12. As per Revelation 21:13 there are a total of twelve gates; just as there are twelve zodiac signs; Then there are exactly 4 sides of the walls of the city, just as there are 4 elements containing three zodiac signs; There are also 3 gates on each of the four sides of the four city walls which totals twelve gates.

13. We have seen the essentiality of air over fire, fire over water and water over earth. All zodiacs are generalized under exactly 4 groups of people. This implies that the world is compiled of mainly 4 different types of people: Air People, Water People, Fire People and Earth People.

14. Relationship-wise it is often almost (but not always) effortless for an Air Person to have a successful relationship with another Air Person because they have a basic compatibility with each other in common as air signs. This is the same for water signs, fire signs and earth signs. With the crossing over of the elements; it seems like air signs can also have a more effortless relationship with fire signs and earth signs can also more effortlessly have good relationships with water signs.

15a. It's been said that the cross overs have logical concepts to substantiate it's logic, as everything in life is grounded in philosophy. The philosophical aspect of the successful union of water and earth is that the earth always meets the ocean; as a matter of fact the earth is at the bottom of each ocean. Air on the other hand compliments fire/energy and contributes to its growth; fire/energy lives in air. Scroll to the following page to see our.. Relationship compatibility chart.

Chapter 5:
The 12 Zodiacs & 4 elements Explained

15b. ———-Zodiac Compatibility Chart ———

01	*Aries 50%*	Leo 97%	Sagittarius 93%	Gemini 83%	Aquarius 78%
02	*Taurus 65%*	Capricorn 98%	Cancer 97%	Virgo 90%	Pisces 85%
03	*Gemini 60%*	Libra 93%	Leo 88%	Aquarius 85%	Aries 83%
04	*Cancer 75%*	Pisces 98%	Taurus 97%	Scorpio 94%	Virgo 90%
05	*Leo 45%*	Ari/Libra 97%	Sagittarius 93%	Gemini 88%	Taurus 73%
06	*Virgo 65%*	Capricorn 95%	Taur/Cancer 90%	Scor/Pisces 88%	Gem/Libra 68%
07	*Libra 75%*	Leo 97%.	Gemini 93%	Aquarius 90%	Pisces 88%
08	*Scorpio 80%*	Pisces 97%	Capricorn 95%	Cancer 94%	Tau/Virgo 88%
09	*Sagittarius 45%*	Aries/Leo 93%	Aquarius 90%	Libra 73%	Gem/Capr 60%
10	*Capricorn 75%*	Taurus 98%	Scorpio 95%	Pisces 88%	Cancer 83%
11	*Aquarius 45%*	Libra/Sag 90%	Gemini 85%	Aries 78%	Scorpio 73%
12	*Pisces 60%*	Cancer 98%	Scorpio 97%	Vir/Libr/Capr 88%	Aries 67%

This chart by no means predetermines whether a relationship will be successful or not, it rather displays the levels of compatibility in all that contributes to a lesser effort needed for harmony of both parties.

Chapter 5:
The 12 Zodiacs & 4 elements Explained

16. The summary of the 4 elements are as follows
- Air Signs (Sanguine) are intellectual and curious
- Fire Signs (Choleric) are Passionate and Exuberant
- Water Signs (Phlegmatic) are Intuitive and Emotional
- Earth Signs (Melancholic) are Practical and Grounded

See the Zodiac's Individual Characteristics Chart below:

17a. —— Zodiac Characteristics Chart ————-

Libras: Are Cardinal Air Signs who are extremely Intelligent, social, agreeable and honest persons who believe strongly in the importance of justice and has supreme conglomerate leadership skills. Because of their ability to manage multiple corporations, they are known to be the most powerful and successful masculine zodiac sign. This confirms why this zodiac produces the majority of billionaires world wide. Their seemingly indecisive attitude is in reality their strategized analytic approach to their plan of action. Their weaknesses is in their ability to be vain and vindictive. Erogenous zones are their backs and butt.
Aquarians: Are Fixed Air Signs and are clever, witty, analytical, technical, truthful, assertive, confident, progressive and innovative. They like to solve problems, improve what's already working well and push boundaries. They are activists, campaigners and progressors of the causes they think will make a difference to the world. Their erogenous zone are their calves and ankles
Geminis: Are Mutable Air Signs who are flexible, extroverted, clever and exciting to be around. They can be indecisive, impulsive, inquisitive, talkative and like making constructive changes. Their positive mutable nature is a great contributive factor to successful leadership skills. Gently stroke their inner arm; Their erogenous zone is their inner arm.

Chapter 5:
The 12 Zodiacs & 4 elements Explained

17b —— Zodiac Characteristics Chart ————-

Cancers: Are Cardinal Water Signs who are very emotional, family oriented, nurturing, highly intuitive, sensitive and insecure at times. They are very spiritually connected and are powerful leaders of a family-like setting; fully aware and caring of the needs and ailments of those they are connected to. Their erogenous zone is their chest or breast.
Scorpios: Are Fixed Water Signs who are very discreet, secretive and mysterious. They are also fearless, bold, passionate, creative, fierce, and very jealous. They are the most sensual of the zodiacs. Their erogenous zone is anywhere that is touched.
Pisces: Are Mutable Water Signs who are very compassionate, artistic, deeply emotional, empathic with some powerful psychic / spiritual gifts, often seeing into the spirit realm. They are often inclined to be extra caring for others. Foot massages; Their erogenous zone is their feet
Arians: Are Cardinal Fire Signs who are by nature the most naturally physically inclined persons of the zodiac; passionate, motivated and confident; they are the ideal kings and queens who like things their way; as they are not the highest in teamwork and social networking, they would do best to run a business or corporation where they are the only ones at the top. Head massages; Their erogenous zone is their head
Leos: Are Fixed Fire Signs who are very proud, confident and like to be the center of attraction. They are prone to follow through with whatever they started. They can be irritable and short tempered and like to do things their way. Their erogenous zone is their spine (Back)

Chapter 5:
The 12 Zodiacs & 4 elements Explained

17c. ——— Zodiac Characteristics Chart ————-

Sagittarians: Are Mutable Fire Signs who are free spirited, lively, passionate, smart, philosophical and like to play by their own rules and regulations. They love travelling, adventure and exploring. Their erogenous zone is their thighs and hips.
Capricorns: Are Cardinal Earth Signs who are known to be the most powerful feminine cardinal sign; a leader with the power to lead in a detailed manner. Capricorns are overachievers; persistent, consistent, practical, and sensitive. They're known to be hard workers who place their work and career above everything. They however place much time and effort in their relationships. Their erogenous zones are their lower back, back of their knees and butt.
Tauruses: Are Fixed Earth Signs who are very dignified, graceful and reliable workers. They are prone to be stubborn, heady and set in their ways, but very good listeners and reliable employees; They are the most prominent in seeing tasks through to completion. They are also known for high sexual stamina and endurance. Their erogenous zone is their neck.
Virgos: Are Mutable Earth Signs who are usually detailed perfectionists, are also very practical and industrious persons who would rather not be the center of attraction. Although humble in appearance, they can be very deceptive at times. They are quick methodical thinkers and often very kind and sympathetic as well. Their erogenous zone is their waist.

Chapter 6:
Our 4 Core Characters

1. Each of the four elements; Air, Fire, Water and Earth are comparable to the 4 core character types known as Sanguine, Phlegmatic, Choleric and Melancholic.
Indeed there are 4 basic different types of personalities, everyone can be identified with one, as one as well as a combination of two or more.
2. People are usually tested by a psychologist to determine what their core characters are. It identifies the core of what your personality is so as to determine what your strengths and weaknesses are. The number "4" provides a very solid structure for our lives as humans living on planet earth; Just as there are "4" Basic personality types (Core characters), there are "4" cardinal directions (East, West, North + South)
3. Then there are the "4" elements of the zodiac signs, then there are "4" corners of the earth with "4" angels standing (Revelation 7:1), there are "4" parts to music (lead, tenor, baritone and bass). 4 being my favorite number is to me the symbol of equality; as a square is built of 4 equal sides as well as the holy city is built with 4 equal sides, of which each side has 3 gates (Revelation 21:16).
4. The interesting factor about the four elements, four directions, four core characters, four seasons "and" four corners we just mentioned, is that they are all interwoven: The 4 core characters, the 4 elements and the 4 cardinal directions are all "one". On the following page, a specific chart is designed to illustrate how they are all connected.
5. The first column of the chart on the following page displays the four elements of the zodiacs. The second column displays the four seasons to match each zodiac. The four core characters of the third row matches the four elements as well as the four seasons the elements represents whereas the fourth columns depict the characteristics of the four core characters defined.

Chapter 6:
Our 4 Core Characters

5. —— Chart of 4 Signs, Seasons & Characters ——-

4. Signs	4. Season	4. Characters	4.Definitions
Fire Signs *Aries* *Leo* *Sagittarius*	*Represents* ***Spring***	**Choleric**	Extroverted: Short tempered, high energy and easily irritable, likes to be in charge and get things done their way.
Water Signs *Cancer* *Scorpio* *Pisces*	*Represents* ***Summer***	**Phlegmatic**	Introverted: Relaxed and peaceful. Prefers a secure job and clarifications on what to do and be relied upon to do so.
Air Signs *Libra* *Aquarius* *Gemini*	*Represents* ***Autumn***	**Sanguine**	Extroverted: Generally enthusiastic, active and social with good communication skills, can get people to do things for them; good leadership skills
Earth Signs *Capricorn* *Taurus* *Virgo*	*Represents* ***Winter***	**Melancholic**	Introverted: Analytical, wise and quiet, able to observe keenly and make wise observations, statements and decisions

6. Core characters may also be described as underlying characters. There are times although a person is a fire sign and is expected to have a choleric character, they may appear to be melancholic on the surface. Sometimes their core character may only be revealed amongst their family or close friends. Sometimes they may function as an extrovert despite what they are at their core; These differences can stem from day of birth as well as birth numerological value as per chapter 12.

Chapter 6:
Our 4 Core Characters

7. I've met persons who would tell me that they are phlegmatic but function like a melancholic, or visa versa. In the typical world of psychology, psychological tests are made in order to determine if a person is phlegmatic, melancholic, choleric or sanguine; Although it may be determined psychologically how a particular individual functions, I do believe in the concept that the elements of the zodiacs determine the character of individuals at core.
8. The energetic fire signs; the primary season of the year seem to have that burst of energy to get things done; a high energetic, no nonsense mentally is ideally the kind of mentality to get things going. This level of determination to get things going however has a low level tolerance for wasting of time or team work. They like things to be done their way and are very easy to lose their cool if their passion to achieve their goals and aspirations is obstructed.
9. The emotionally driven water signs; are the type of people who can get the tedious routine work done. They generally do not care to be in charge of anything or anyone. They'd rather keep a low profile, be shown what they need to do and be left alone to get it done for the time they were scheduled to do so. Their general demeanor can be just show me what to do and until what time and let me be: Ideal chore characteristic of a phlegmatic .
10. The rather free spirited air signs are typically sanguine by core; They have the power to talk their way in or out of any situation. They were born socially skilled and able to communicate really well. Their ability to master team work makes them some of the world's wealthiest people; This explains why the vast majority of the world's billionaires are known to be typically air signs.
11. Earth signs are melancholic and known to be very detailed perfectionists. They are very efficient with time and productivity. They, like the water signs, prefer to be unnoticed and would normally guide things from behind the....

Chapter 6:
Our 4 Core Characters

.... scenes. They are like the wise owls of the zodiacs: They don't speak much but are very analytical, they pay keen attention to everything that is being said or done and usually can come up with great input after comparing the perspectives of everyone. They are also primarily detailed workers and make excellent mathematicians, auditors or accountants.

12. Amongst the four core characters, none is better than the other, as all are 4 gigantic pieces of the same puzzle that needs to be fit together in order to acquire optimal productivity. As each element has a different perspective to life, it is ideal to establish a board of directors with each of these elements with ideally an air element chairman to review and decide based on the perspective of each in a democratic manner, as air signs thrive on justice.

13. Because earth signs are so detailed and cautious of errors, a double input of them could stagnate the movement of a board with constructive but excessive critique. A double input of water signs, whose spirituality is superior, may make decisions based on emotions and may compromise productivity of a board. A double input of the fire element may be too intense for the smooth flow of progress.

14. Air signs however may be double with one to analyze all perspectives in order to decipher how to combine all their strengths and the other to establish that all things are possible. Too much air however will self destruct with a group of go getters who would do anything without hesitating. Balance is acquired from the uniting of all; when all the elements are combined, we become supernaturally powerful and productive.

15. I recalled being a guest speaker at a conference back in 2017, where I used a very great analogy of a roof and the walls and their contributions to a building. I remember stating that walls combined and tied together create ....

Chapter 6:
Our 4 Core Characters

.... a very strong bond for a structure and that without a roof it would be a ruin. I also concurred that there can be no roof without the walls wherewith to support it. Without the roof you have no building, but it's completely impossible to have a roof if there are no walls to support it.

16. We can therefore see the philosophical aspects of the elements in that Fire sign people are passionate and consume their environment with their presence. Water signs are emotionally adaptable to their surroundings they are placed into. Air signs do not like to be contained, comparable to not liking to be restricted to what they can or cannot do whilst earth signs are grounded and like to make decisions based on what is factual.

17. If we were to apply these four elements into a business; look at the logic of how their roles may be applied from all angles: A cardinal air sign (sanguine) as director, a fire sign (choleric) as general manager, a melancholic as supervisor and phlegmatic as executioner (s). The air sign who hates conflict assigns the fire sign as general manager, who has zero tolerance level for nonsense or complacency. The fire sign then assigns the detailed melancholic supervisor to ensure that the phlegmatic routine worker executes his/her tasks exactly as is required.

18. Because of the air sign's dislike for conflict, he/she will strategically avoid confronting anyone for what he/she dislikes. His/her appointing of the choleric fire sign manager is so appropriate, in that the fire sign is confrontational and doesn't condone complacency in any form. Because the earth sign is so very detailed, it would be very rare for a professional conflict to occur between the two. The fire sign will be very detailed in relaying what is needed to be done in a very detailed manner to the water sign (Phleg).

19. The typical water sign who is by nature phlegmatic may prefer a routine job, whereby he/she doesn't have ....

Chapter 6:
Our 4 Core Characters

.... to carry the burden of responsibility and can be free at the end of their work shift to pursue their other hobbies without having to worry about their function at the work place. The sanguine air sign director is then ideal to do the marketing himself as he can talk his way into getting clients to make his business successful.

20. It is imperative to understand that no element is more important than the other and that any of them can be the director. They would however have to adapt appropriately in how the organizational chart is established.

Now if peradventure the water sign phlegmatic were to be the director, he/she would be wise to hire a cardinal air sign sanguine assistant director to also hold the position of marketing director for the acquisition of clients to ensure a successful business.

21. The assistant director (cardinal sanguine) who will also function in the position of marketing director, can have a choleric general manager who in turn has a melancholic supervisor who supervises phlegmatic laborers. It is very likely however that the phlegmatic director would report to work every day and establish routine tasks despite him/her being the director, because of the nature of his/her chore character.

22. A melancholic director will be a very hands on director who will often participate in the daily functioning of the work. He/she will take pride in saying; “I need to be a part of what is going on in order for it to run smoothly”. Which is why they make excellent supervisors: They have the power to do as well as the power to oversee. They too would do well to have a cardinal air sign assistant director, Choleric manager, melancholic supervisor and phlegmatic executioners.

23. Same goes for the choleric fire sign director; Air sign assistant director, choleric manager, melancholic super....

Chapter 6:
Our 4 Core Characters

....visor and phlegmatic executioners. Let us now explore the reason why every element is so appropriate for each role; Air signs are born with the underlying power to be great communicators, they know how to talk, influence and communicate with people. They are the ones who are more prone to get people to do what they want, as they are naturally gifted with the art of how to stay neutral with everyone; they love peace and harmony and would go a long way to acquire it.

24. Air signs seem to come over as indecisive, but are not: they prefer to be on good terms with everyone and prefer to show the valid points everyone may have. Air signs are very charming smooth talkers and are the best at influencing people, which is very handy for marketing and financial growth in business, which makes them very good for keeping harmony in a business. Let us give an example: a choleric no nonsense manager and a phlegmatic routine worker got into a physical brawl, whereas the phleg fell asleep on the desk and the choleric hit him:

25. The phleg got angry and struck back the manager and it comes to the sanguine director to resolve. The director may call in the choleric manager by himself and tell him how glad he is that he's following up on the workers to ensure that they're doing their job and what an asset he is to the company and will dwell ninety percent on that. In a trivial ten percent he would say; the only thing maybe for the next time you can shake him rather than hit him.

26. The choleric manager would leave the office appreciated and valued, yet reminded not to hit. The air sign director as the great communicator will then call in the phleg who was sleeping, by himself and say; I know you must've been tired that you fell asleep on the job, as I know you wouldn't have done it intentionally. The phleg being emotional may break ....

Chapter 6:
Our 4 Core Characters

.... in tears claiming how no one knows what he's going through and explain to the sanguine director what was going on in his/her life after which he'll see the sanguine director as his best friend. After he vents the sanguine director may tell him he'll give him 2 days off with pay privately to allow him some rest.

27. The sanguine director may after bring both into a meeting and say how in general we all work well together and look forward to overlooking the misunderstanding and everything runs smoothly after. The sanguine air sign people and communication skills are the ultimate source of acquiring wealth as well as harmony which in actuality goes hand in hand. Whilst the choleric fire sign manager may not have the patience for that, everything would fall apart eventually without them as everyone will become more and more complacent until the company becomes stagnant in productivity.

28. The melancholic supervisor is probably the most essential person to keep a company going if it is imperative to downsize drastically to function on a skeleton staff. Melancholics are like the wise old owl who see in depth of situations but also have the power to function in any capacity; from managerial to routine. They are very diligent, consistent and extremely reliable by core. They may not be the ones to invent the wheel. As a director, they are not likely to change things but can be relied upon to execute exactly as instructed and may not be prone to change unless directly from an authorized person.

29. The phlegmatic routine worker is last but not least; they are by core very spiritual and may see things that no one else sees; they are capable of doing routine work because its done from a very spiritual perspective. The routine job does not affect them as it would an air sign, due to the fact that their minds are generally very occupied and are able to establish a pattern of work that ....

Chapter 6:
Our 4 Core Characters

.... allows their minds to roam whilst executing their tasks in a very zen like manner.

30. Phlegmatic routine workers are the most vital to keep a business going and are usually in the majority. They are comparable to the blocks (which are the most in abundance) that are placed together to establish a wall to make it possible to have a roof. The melancholic supervisors are like the foundation the walls are built upon whereas the choleric manager is comparable to the steel that ties in the walls together. This leaves the sanguine director who is the roof of the building.

31. To further comprehend that everyone is relevant, please note the following: The blocks (phlegmatic routine workers) which comprise the walls, will sink if there is no solid foundation to rest upon. The very roof will collapse eventually if the foundation is weak. Its often stated in the bible that a house's foundation (melancholic supervisors) should be built upon a rock (solid).

32. On the other hand, if there is no steel (choleric manager) to tie the foundation, walls (phlegmatic routine workers) and roof (sanguine director) together, the entire building with also collapse. Without the roof, the entire building will be deemed a ruin. Trees will grow inside, all equipment will get wet and rot away eventually. God designed everyone (all four core characters) to fit perfectly into the puzzle to complete the harmony of the world we live in.

33. A sanguine director, may not have the power to handle a phlegmatic routine worker's job, nor does a phlegmatic routine worker have the vision of the sanguine director. The demand to have to ensure that salaries are paid to everyone at month's end will be overbearing for the phlegmatic routine worker. The sanguine director's job is to envision and implement new concepts to increase revenue as well as to keep up with the changes in technology, which will allow the business to thrive.

Chapter 6:
Our 4 Core Characters

34. We spent some time reviewing how the four core characters can fit into a work environment. Let us now take the time to review the analogy of how appropriately they fit into an advisory board. The fire sign board member, who might be ideal as secretary of the board is a great initiator to get things going; take minutes and organize meetings etc. The water sign board member is ideal as a general member whereas the melancholic earth sign may be the best option to be treasurer as they're so detailed with everything.
35. One cardinal sanguine air sign board member may make and ideal chairman to weigh the odds of the best choices and the other sanguine air sign would be ideal to cast a vote into an optimistic outcome. Why was each element/chore character assigned to a particular role would be a question posed: Here's a generalized version of the answer.
36. Choleric fire signs are highly energetic and driven, they would be relentless in ensuring to organize the board meetings and relaying the meeting minutes, hence they're very appropriate to be secretary of the board aka Administrative Director. Phlegmatic water signs are emotional which is the core of intuitive and very spiritually powerful; they have the capacity to sense things without evidence, therefore ideal as a general board member to tip the scales to ensure the right decisions are executed.
37. Sanguine air signs are very influential by core; they have the gift of people skills. They have the core capacity to lead with harmony. Choleric fire signs are also leaders, but not as harmonious or team players as air signs. Choleric fire signs function best as the single head of an organization or the sole captain of one ship. In a group setting the cardinal sanguine air element would be ideal as president / chairman / general director.
38. A board should preferably consist of 3,5 or 7 mem….

Chapter 6:
Our 4 Core Characters

....bers in order to be able to vote democratically for a choice or preference of action. Although a board can be formed with 3 persons: President, Secretary and Treasure; it will weaken it's potential by not having the 4 core characters to put their ideas together in order to acquire the best possible decisions, whereby the president can tip the scale, should the decision be a close call.

39. The melancholic earth sign, who is very grounded and practical will often look at the reasons why not to do something, whereas the sanguine air sign has an almost complete optimistic perspective on just about anything. They often look at all the reasons why anything can be done. Again I remind you that we're talking core, oftentimes many people develop a character that overrides their core character, as the means of cardinality also entails day of birth as well as numerology.

40. This is why some people may say, I am phlegmatic but I function like a melancholic. From a philosophical perspective, we can also compare the four core characters to the four parts of music. To those of you who are familiar with cappella singing; you may know that there are typically four parts in a cappella group; The lead, tenor, baritone and bass. These four parts of the voice are also found in musical compositions; two in treble clef and two in the bass clef.

41. I think its fair to compare the lead part to the sanguine air sign, whereas lead is what sets the melody or I may say is the initiator of the song and can be considered extroverted. The tenor which is the highest part is so comparable to choleric, which may stand out most as the highest part tends to be most vocal, comparable to being extroverted. The baritone is ideally the typical phlegmatic water sign that is barely heard but blends in so smoothly to enrich the song and is all the way introverted. The bass vocalist is Melancholic; an introverted, grounded earth sign.

Chapter 6: Our 4 Core Characters

42. Being a bass vocalist myself, I am very accustomed to singing the deepest part of the four vocals; I must agree how appropriate it is to compare the melancholic earth sign to the bass vocal. The melancholic person is an introvert, which means they seldom speak out, but when they do speak out, it is with great power and wisdom after having analyzed everyone's perspective over a long period of time. This is so similar to the bass vocalist who only shines out on certain parts of a song, but when he does, it is very powerful and exciting to hear.

43. To compare the tenor to the choleric fire signs is also on point in my opinion. Fire so appropriately depicts choleric as well. They are the no none sense, high energy type of people who are very extroverted and can share their thoughts whether good or bad on the spur of the moment. In my opinion the most beautiful part of a song is when the tenor is able to go very high. The high part in a song is comparable to seasoning in food. Hence the choleric's energy is comparable to the seasoning in food; the tenor.

44. In bringing closure to this chapter with regards to the four core characters, we can conclude that the four core characters; melancholic, phlegmatic, choleric and sanguine are all comparable to the four zodiac elements of earth, water, fire and air; which are in turn comparable to the musical parts; bass, baritone, tenor and lead, which are comparable to the four cardinal directions; east, west, north and south. Isn't it amazing how structured and organized everything was orchestrated ? Doesn't this confirm the presence of the higher power?

Chapter 7:
The Three Modules Explained

1. The word module means of a set of.. or independent units that can be used to construct a more complex structure, such as an item of furniture for the building of ships which are now built in modules rather than in a whole from the base up. In general module simply means sections. The modules of the zodiac signs are the three divisions of the four elements; hence the term modules.
2. The twelve zodiac signs are divided into their compilation of the four elements. These four elements in sequence are; summer, spring, autumn and winter. As we recall from chapter five, each element consists of three zodiac signs: The fire signs (Choleric) which represented summer were; Aries, Leo and Sagittarius. The water signs (Phlegmatic) which represent spring were; Pisces, Cancer and Scorpio. The air signs (Sanguine) which represent autumn were; Aquarius, Gemini and Libra.
3. The division of each element are called modules. Each of the four elements consists of three modules. The names of the three modules are; initiators also known as cardinal signs, fixed signs and mutable signs. This means that water signs have three modules, earth signs have three modules, fire signs have three modules and air signs also have three modules that carry the same names (Cardinal, Fixed and Mutable).
4. The next three chapters to follow will give an intimate break down of the three modules, which are listed above as the cardinal, fixed and mutable signs. These three modules are the ones to provide each one of the three characteristics needed for all humans to fulfill the tasks appropriately necessary for our planet's smooth functioning. We need some people to establish ideas (initiators), we need another set of people to be able to execute the ideas, then we need another set of people to establish supporting ideas in order to be able progress with the manner in which things are done.

Chapter 7: The Three Modules Explained

5. If everyone on earth was busy creating ideas, then there would be no one with the capacity to execute them. Yet if there is no one to create supporting ideas, our progress on earth as humans would become stagnant. For a more vivid example let us return to the past when cardinal people presumably discovered the pen and established a way to write the financial accountability of business on old pieces of paper bags which the fixed signs executed.
6. Let's presume a mutable person discovered a way to clip the papers together in a date pattern, which made it easier for accountability to be established. Then lets say some years later, another cardinal discovered the note book and a majority of fixed signs maintained the notes in the note book. A cardinal then discovers the accounting system in the computer era as a mutable brings excel as an option to upgrade from the notebook to excel.
7. This routine can continue with mutable signs upgrading from excel to quick books pro after a cardinal managed to create the quick books program from excel. The cardinal signs are the initiators, the fixed signs are the executioners whereas the mutable signs bring changes by adaptation. Positive mutable signs bring positive changes whereas negative mutable signs can destroy what is already established; bare in mind that our gifts can be used for good or bad. May we therefore always strive to be good and optimistic.
8. Cardinals are the initiators, fixed the consistent routine doers and mutable signs are the contributors to change for adaptability. The contributions of mutable signs do not have to be oppositional if or when derived from a positive mind. In fact their input is usually the icing on the cake. May we ever strive to be a positive vibration in our allotted contributing gifts to the world.

Chapter 8:
The Four Cardinal Signs Explained

1. The word cardinal means front runner, initiator or simply leader. Cardinal people are those whose zodiac signs are either Aries, Cancer, Libra, Capricorn or were born on a Wednesday or cardinal "or" master number despite their zodiac sign.
Aries, the first sign of the zodiac is the cardinal fire sign; one of the 3 fire signs (along with Leo and Sagittarius) whom we identified as choleric chore characters.
Cancer, the 4th sign of the zodiac is the cardinal of the water signs (along with Pisces and Scorpio) whom we identified as the phlegmatic core characters.
2. Libra is the 7th sign of the zodiac and is the cardinal of the air signs and one of the three other air signs (along with Aquarius and Gemini) whom we identified as the sanguine core characters. Capricorn is the 10th sign of the zodiac and is the cardinal of the earth sings (along with Taurus and Virgo) whom we identified as the melancholic core characters.
3. Cardinal signs (Aries, Cancer, Libra and Capricorn are referred to as the leaders of the zodiacs; the initiators. They are the ones to invent things or make things happen. They are often usually the ones to come up with the grand ideas that make a change in various eras if credit is given to the right person. Wednesday born people are also cardinal despite their zodiac signs. Just as midday is when the sun is at it's highest peak in the sky (noon), Wednesday is also when a week is at its highest peak.
4. We will take time to address the Wednesday borns in our final chapter of this book as we continue with the cardinals of the zodiac. I will now endeavor to share my perspective of the cardinals in sequence. The reason why we start with Aries, is because it launches spring and spring is supposedly the beginning season of the year when everything comes back to life after the stagnation of the winter season to end the zodiac year.

Chapter 8: The Four Cardinal Signs Explained

5. Each cardinal sign launches the beginning of a season whereas each fixed sign carries the season and each mutable sign ends each season. We can rephrase the concept and say that each cardinal sign "leads" a season to commence whereas each fixed sign upkeeps the season and every mutable signs terminates a season. Aries is the cardinal season because it launches/leads the season into spring; It's when trees come back to life and animals come out of hibernation etc.

6. Remember that astrology is the effect or influence the planets have on the earth. Just as plants grow in accordance with the moon and turtles can be caught laying eggs on the shore with the full moon: the magnitude of our gifts allotted to us humans are in affiliation with the timing of what part of which season the planets govern, that we were born into; beginning, middle or end. This is more evidence of a Divine Power implementation of structure for our behalf.

7. Cardinal sign Aries is very powerful: The Aries cardinal fire sign people are more physically inclined than average.; to the extent that in Greek Mythology Aries is referred to as the god of war. This makes sense as spring is the season of rebirth where nature uses force to bring trees back to life, lets the grass grow back and leaves grow back on the trees. The beginning of the spring season is also when the creatures that hibernated can come out of hibernation. Spring is truly a powerful season.

8. The cardinal Aries people are powerful leaders but function best alone; they prefer to do things their way. Teamwork is not their forte. It is also interesting to know that the typical Aries sensitive zone is their head, and they do indeed represent the head. The A in Aries is typically a timely representation of alpha, meaning the beginning. Head massages for Aries people is ideally soothing to them.

Chapter 8:
The Four Cardinal Signs Explained

9. The Aries Cardinal Fire (Choleric) people are extroverted, masculine signs who are very determined and fixated on achieving their goals they have set out to do, so similar to nature in spring using its creative power to bring everything to life. Governed by the planet of Mars, Aries' power lies in it's passion and its commitment to itself and functions best alone. They are great entrepreneurs and at times may be prone to start too many projects and may need to return to complete, but they do have the power to do so.

10. The Cancer cardinal water (phlegmatic) sign is governed by the moon and is an introverted, feminine sign that is very emotionally connected and spiritually in tune. Cancers are ideal leaders for smaller corporations with a family like setting. Cancers are usually up to date with their employees ailments and their personal issues and shows a higher level of care and concern to their wellbeing.

11. The Libra cardinal air sign (sanguine) is a masculine, extroverted leader of the zodiac. Librans are very skilled in communicating with people and have the capacity to get almost anyone to do just about anything. For this reason Librans are considered an extreme cardinal sign and produces the highest percentage of billionaires worldwide. Librans who are high on justice are ideal for presidents of boards or directors of organizations and are capable of running a conglomerate (a vast variety of business at once).

12. The laid back attitude in Librans which come over as inconsistency is often an analytical approach to what has to be done. Librans analyze, after which they spring into action with a confirmed source of direction. Librans weakness is that they can be very vindictive and hold grudges for a long time prior to executing justice. Governed by the planet Venus, Libra is high on looking good ....

Chapter 8:
The Four Cardinal Signs Explained

.... and being in love and are known to be the most romantic people of the zodiac.

13. The cardinal Capricorn earth sign (melancholic) has a large gap between its fellow earth signs. It is the other introverted but extreme powerful feminine sign of the zodiac . They are extremely great leaders who have the power to run a business in a very detailed manner of excellence. A single business run by a Capricorn is likely to bypass the quality of expectations. Their only setback is that because of how detailed they are, they don't have the capacity as cardinal Libra to run a conglomerate. However, neither can the Libran meet the high standards of excellence that Capricorn can achieve singularly.

14. If a business is left in a Capricorn's hand to manage without any assistance; they have the capacity to manage and handle the routine work simultaneously by core. Libra on the other hand has the power to lead and run conglomerates but does not by core exhibit the power to do the work themselves. Conglomerates however simply mean a multiple group of companies, which is the ability to multitask from a business perspective with various business or branches. Unlike the Caps, Librans would be in need of the fixed signs in order to produce.

15. As we bring closure to this chapter, it is imperative that I illustrate that each Cardinal Sign represents a spiritual number. Aries is the number one, Cancer is the fourth , Libra is the seventh whilst Capricorn is the tenth "1" God, "4" directions, 4 corners to the city, 4 corners of the earth...7 days of a week, 7 candle sticks, 10 toes, 10 fingers, 10 commandments

Chapter 9:
The Four Fixed Signs Explained

1. The word fixed speaks for itself, it means focused or fixated on the task ahead. Fixed signs are the doers of the zodiac; these are the ones who have the power to execute that which was established by the Cardinals. The fixed signs are the powerhouses who maintain things or keep things going. The Fixed signs establish consistency and durability in all areas of their expertise. Is it of any surprise that these grounded earth sign people "do not" welcome change?

2. Protocol has already been established that the fixed zodiac signs are Aquarius' (of the air signs), Leos (of the fire signs), Scorpios (of the water signs) and Taurus' (of the earth signs). Remember air signs are deemed Sanguine as underlying, Fire signs are deemed choleric as underlying, water signs are deemed Phlegmatic as underlying and earth signs are deemed Melancholic as underlying.

3. These signs are fixed in their field of their underlying expertise. Once protocol has been established, it is not likely that anyone will convince the fixed signs to change anything. Howbeit, it is important to know that the fixed Fire sign Leo can have a more passionate nature as its core element is choleric, the fixed air sign Aquarius may have a more free spirited nature as it's core is sanguine, the fixed water sign Scorpio may have a more laid back nature as its core element is water.

4. Earth signs are the most fixed of all the fixed signs as they are by nature the "hands on" people . They are by nature more detailed than the rest of the zodiacs . They are generally more diligent, grounded and practical than all the other signs and are therefore the chief of the fixed signs. The fixed earth sign Taurus therefore will be very committed and dedicated to his/her task. They are capable of undertaking the most difficult tasks that would break the other fixed signs of the zodiacs.

Chapter 9: The Four Fixed Signs Explained

5. The Fixed Fire sign Leo comes with the fiery nature of passion at its core and is also very intense in completing whatever tasks that it has set out to do. The combination of the passion of fire with the fixated spirit of the Lion is a force to reckon with. This fixed fire sign is very determined in completing what it has set out or was assigned to do with a high level of intensity. Because the fire element in itself is so strong and passionate at its core, even the fixed and mutable fire signs are very much sub cardinal by nature and exhibit leadership qualities.
6. The choleric underlying character of the fire element in leo can be very dominant and likes to do things his way. They can become easily angry, aggressive and impulsive to have things done a certain way, or as was requested to do. The lion however likes to be the center of attraction and can be the life or center of attraction at a party with the strong extroverted character that they possess. They prefer to do things at their pace, but yet would impulsively want others to comply with their timing as to when to do what.
7. The fixed water sign Scorpio is ideally phlegmatic, very laid back and prefers to do routine stuff without having to be mentally challenged. A fixed water sign Scorpio could easily be heard saying, I don't want to be in charge of anything and don't wish to work overtime; Just tell me what I have to do and leave me alone to do it and allow me to leave at my scheduled time . This fixated water sign can execute routine tasks that could easily bore or tire out a mutable or cardinal person mentally.
8. It is of no relevance if their job is a high end job or a basic job of lifting a security boom to let cars into a residential area or a heart surgeon in the intensive care, they can organize their minds to handle the routine tasks of any capacity and stay focused. They often have a hobby that they do each day after work that gives them a spiritual....

Chapter 9:
The Four Fixed Signs Explained

....sense of fulfillment or enlightenment, as we know the water signs are the most spiritual and emotional signs of the entire zodiac. Many water signs need a structure and routine form of functioning. A multi millionaire who doesn't need to work, could easily be seen reporting to work each day, establishing the necessary structure for their lives.

9. Air signs are the masterminds of the zodiac, they are the great thinkers and philosophers. They are probably are the least hands on persons of the zodiac which is likely because they are the thinkers, the ones with great minds. They are good at communicating, reasoning and getting people to do whatever they desire with charm and strategic approach methods. Fixed air signs are great visionaries and are ideal to assign to projects and come up with ideas to keep it going

10. Fixed signs as was mentioned earlier are the doers, the backbone of many companies and organizations who often do not get enough credit for the consistent hard work that they do to keep things going. It is imperative to give credit to the fixed, reliable persons within our organizations who deal with tedious challenges to keep things running..hats off to you fixed people, our heroes.

The Fixed Signs

♎	♌	♏	♒
Taurus	Leo	Scorpio	Aquarius
Spring	Summer	Autumn	Winter
Earth	Fire	Water	Air

Chapter 10:
The Four Mutable Signs Explained

1. The term "mutable" comes from the Latin root mutables, which means change, and as expected, it is related to the English words "mutate" and "mutation." If you are a mutable sign, **you are considered an adaptable chameleon, which means you can shift into many forms and take on different personas**. A mutable person ends the season and can adapt to situations as needed. A negative mutable may also be very unnecessarily oppositional to the way things are being done and disrupt progress without a substantial cause.
2. Mutable people however are the ones who can bring about the adaptable changes and flexibility needed to accommodate unexpected situations that were not catered for. Mutable forces can also upgrade into the changes of society. Mutable persons are flexible and can implement changes to keep up with the changes in time. They are the ones to keep things up to date in a society that is ever changing.
3. A company may be stuck in the past using the note book e.g. for accountability, whilst the fixed person isn't too fond of changes, a mutable may bring the upgrade option to the director who will later establish its upgraded use and enhance the company's productivity and accountability. A negative or pessimistic mutable person however can be exceptionally controversial; For every suggestion made they may create a reason why it wouldn't work.
4. Our mutable signs are Virgos of the earth signs, Pisces of the water signs, Sagittarius of the fire signs and Gemini of the air signs. One's core character is one's "underlying" character. This can be overridden by what circumstances could've made anyone to become, cardinal day or numerology. Howbeit, critics as well as leaders can be found in just about any zodiac, despite the core. Mutable people are at the end of each season and ....

Chapter 10:
The Four Mutable Signs Explained

...are the ones who bring an end to an old era in order for the Cardinals to start a new season or era.

5. Mutable persons compliment the entire zodiac as they all fit into each other for the best possible timing and results. The Cardinal persons, Fixed Persons and Mutable persons are designed to provide optimum productivity; They complete each other; The initiator, the activator and the adapter.

6. Mutable persons are the powerful adaptable people of the zodiac who can be flexible and adaptable to change, without them things would crash as life is very unpredictable and subject to change. The stability of the fixed, initiating skills of the Cardinal and the adaptability of the mutable united as a force of one makes an invincible team. We show much respect to the powerful mutable signs of the zodiac

7. Air Gemini will have core leadership mutable skills, Earth Virgos have hands on detailed mutable skills, Fire Sagittarius have adventurous mutable skills and Water Pisces has emotional, intuitive and spiritual mutable skills. What a powerful team that compliments the absolute best results should they unite and function as a force of one.

Chapter 11:
The Four Seasons Explained

1. Before understanding the zodiacs I used to wonder what the bible meant when mentioning about the four corners of the earth as well as the twelve tribes of the earth. I now realize that the four corners of the earth has four cardinal directions from which the four seasons are derived; Spring, Summer Autumn and Winter. As per Revelation 21:10 to 13 there are 4x3 gates from each cardinal direction to the new capital city of the world for citizens of the entire planet to have access to.

2. As per Genesis 1;14 it is confirmed that the planets (which are referred to as lights) are there to determine the days, nights, **seasons**, signs and years. Genesis 1:16 specifically says that the greater light (The sun) determines the daytime and the lesser light (The moon) determines the nighttime. The latter part of the same verse 16 refers to the other planets as stars and Psalms 104:19 confirms that the 4 seasons are determined by the moon.

3. It seems as if the moon along with the other planets which are referred to as stars, are what decides the seasons. All the planets seem to be:

I. The Sun: (Sunday) Sun's Day
II. The Moon: (Monday) Moon's Day ..Lunes in Spanish
III. Mars: (Tuesday) Mars' Day..Martes in Spanish
IV. Mercury (Wednesday) Mercury's Day...Miercules in Spanish
V. Jupiter: (Thursday)...Jueves in Spanish
VI. Venus: (Friday)...Viernes in Spanish
VII. Saturn (Saturday)..Sabado in Spanish, which means Sabbath

4. The primary set of planets seem to determine the days whereas it seems the following planets (listed below) collaborate with the moon (as per Psalms 104:19) to determine the seasons:

VIII. Uranus
IX. Neptune ....

Chapter 11:
The Four Seasons Explained

....Another theory posed is that Bible is declaring that the sun determines the day as per its rising and setting from within its chamber. There's the implication that exactly what we see is what it is; it rises in the east, goes overhead, sets in the west and goes under and around to rise in the east again (Psalms 19:5 / Isaiah 45:6).

5. The moon on the other hand circles around exactly as is seen and comes back around; in essence this theory concurs that the moon circles around whereas the sun circles overhead under and around to the same spot within its chamber. As we proceed to decipher our theory of the four seasons, we must first acknowledge that the 4 elements, the 4 cardinal directions, the 4 cardinal zodiac signs and the biblical terminology regarding the 4 corners of the earth are all affiliated and represent each other.

6. Review our chart below which depicts the affiliation of the seasons with its cardinal direction, element, color, race and cardinal number.

Cardinal Season	Cardinal Direction	Element	Color Card Races	Cardinal Number
Spring	East	**Fire**	**Yellow**	1
Summer	South	**Water**	**Black**	4
Autumn	West	**Air**	**Red**	7
Winter	North	**Earth**	**White**	10

7. Revelation 7:1 depicts 4 angels standing at the four corners of the earth, which seems to divide the world into 4 sectors. Revelation 7:4-8 now lists the tribes under the following names that will be stipulated in the chart on the subsequent page. The first column depicts the tribes in order of the old testament; the actual sons whereas Revelation 17:4-8 trades the name of Dan to Manasseh. Seems the reason for this is that God divides the world ...

Chapter 11:
The Four Seasons Explained

….into 4 quarters, but each quarter has 3 tribes; 4x3 equals the twelve tribes of the earth. This explains why in Revelation 21:13 confirms that there are 3 gates on each side of the New Capital city of the world, to enable citizens to access the city from "all" directions.

8. Our chart below depicts the names of the 12 tribes from which symbolically 12000 are saved from each tribe, totaling 144000.

Nrs	*Old Testament 12 Tribes*	*Rev. 12 Tribes By Age*	*Rev. 12 Tribes By Sequence*	
01	Reuben	Reuben	Judah	12,000.00
02	Simeon	Simeon	Reuben	12,000.00
03	*Levi*	Levi	*Gad*	12,000.00
04	*Judah*	Judah	*Asher*	12,000.00
05	**Dan**	**Manasseh**	Naphtali	12,000.00
06	Naphtali	Naphtali	Manasseh	12,000.00
07	Gad	*Gad*	Simeon	12,000.00
08	Asher	*Asher*	Levi	12,000.00
09	Issachar	Issachar	Issachar	12,000.00
10	Zebulon	Zebulon	Zebulon	12,000.00
11	Joseph	Joseph	Joseph	12,000.00
12	Benjamin	Benjamin	Benjamin	12,000.00
				144,000.00

9. God seems to move in a very strong pattern with regards to everything. There are 4 basic races on earth that we can refer to as Yellow (Spring), Black (Summer), Red (Autumn) and White (Winter). Out of these 4 races there are 12 tribes of which the primary 4 are cardinal, hence when the four corners of the world are mentioned ….

Chapter 11:
The Four Seasons Explained

….it is also imperative to remember that each corner has a different season, and just as there are 3 modules for each element and 4x3 is 12, there are 3 sub races under each race as per their sub directions of each cardinal direction.

10. This is the philosophical interpretation of the numbers 3,4 and 12 which are extremely prevalent as well as symbolical. There are 3 gates on each cardinal direction of the city which match the 3 modules of each element. Then there are the 4 seasons that match the 4 corners of the earth and the 4 cardinal directions that match the 4 cardinal races of the earth; Red, Yellow, Black and White. I am certain many of us know the traditional song that goes Jesus love the little children, all the children of the world; Red and Yellow, Black and White, they are precious in his sight.

11. The 4 seasons in sequence are Spring, Summer, Autumn and Winter. Spring is when everything comes back new; the bears and other animals that hibernated come out of hibernation. The trees grow back their leaves and the grass grows back. The frozen rivers now start their flow of water again. It's like a brand new beginning and ideally comparable to when God first created earth. Directly after Spring we get summer, which is the peak of life when everything is blooming. Summer is ended by Autumn when leaves fall from their trees and everything comes to an end.,

12. Autumn is more comparable to a cleansing than to death. The reason why it is a cleaning is because the trees don't die, instead the shed their old leaves in order to come back with new leaves. Winter seems to freeze or preserve things in order to have a renewing of nature. Even the lakes are frozen whereby many can walk on them. When winter is released by Spring we then go back to a new beginning and rebirth.

Chapter 11:
The Four Seasons Explained

13. There are "four" seasons in total: **The first season is called Spring**, and it ranges "approximately" from March 21st until June 20th, which can fluctuate by a day or two in some estimations. Spring is the season to begin projects, open that new business or launch that new book. Your new year resolutions are ideal to establish in Spring, whereas Spring is the actual beginning of the new year; not the dead of winter.
14. Aries is deemed Cardinal because its range is the beginning part of Spring the first month of the Zodiac which commences from March 21st to April 19th. In actuality this should be considered the first month of the year and is the beginning of the season of Spring. Bare in mind that the planets are to determine signs, seasons days and years (Genesis 1:14-19)
15. Because Taurus ranges from April 20th to May 20th; Taurus' dates are in the middle of the season of Spring as we recall that the entire spring season ranges from March 21st thru June 20th. It can be said therefore that Taurus "carries" the season of Spring and is therefore called a fixed sign because it is in the middle of Spring, unlike Gemini who brings and end to the season, with its range from May 21st to June 20th.
16. It can therefore be said that Gemini brings an end to the season of Spring and the reason why it can be said that Gemini is a mutable sign is, as it ends or is at the ending of Spring which (as is listed above) brings an end to the Spring season. So for an overview, let's recap: All signs that are at the beginning of any season are called Cardinal, those that are in the middle are called fixed signs whereas those that are at the end of the season or ends the seasons are called mutable signs.
17. Cardinals are initiators or leaders as they are the beginning, fixed maintain or keep things going whilst ....

Chapter 11: The Four Seasons Explained

....the Mutable signs bring an end or changes to seasons or circumstances. Thus far we can see that there are no great mysteries to understanding astrology and the zodiacs, there is only structure, logic and order.
The logic of people born at the beginning of a season will have a fundamental ability to lead; Those born in the middle of a season have the fundamental ability to maintain, whereas those born at the end of a season have the capacity to establish adaptability for change .

18. As we continue, the second season subsequent to Spring is called Summer. Summer is when everything is at its peak, the sun shines brightest and nature is blooming and at its peak. Trees have leaves and filled with fruit and everyone is up and about. Summer ranges approximately from June 20th throughout September 22nd. The cardinal summer sign which is at the commence of the summer season is called Cancer. The dates for Cancer range from June 22nd throughout July 22nd.

19. The fixed summer sign is the fire sign Leo, which ranges from July 23rd throughout August 22nd. Leo being in the middle of the Summer season is referred to as the fixed fire sign of the summer season. Virgo is now the mutable earth sign that brings an end to the summer season, with its range from August 23rd throughout September 22nd.

20. After summer comes Autumn, which is the third season when everything cleanses itself. The trees shed their leaves and the grass dries up to make preparation for nature to begin to freeze everything. After this will be the fourth and subsequent season called Winter. Autumn ranges from September 23rd throughout December 23rd. The cardinal sign of Autumn is air sign Libra, which ranges from September 23rd throughout October 22nd. The fixed sign of autumn is water sign Scorpio ranging from October 23rd throughout November 21st.

Chapter 11:
The Four Seasons Explained

21. The mutable sign of the autumn is fire sign Sagittarius, which ranges from November 22nd throughout December 21st. Our summary of the autumn season is Cardinal Libra; the air sign. Virgo is the fixed sign after which follows Sagittarius the fire sign.
We will now move on to the fourth and final season, which is winter.
22. Winter which is the fourth and final season, ranges from December 22nd throughout March 19th and is headed by cardinal sign Capricorn. Capricorn ranges from December 22nd throughout January 19th.
The fixed sign of the winter season is air sign Aquarius, which ranges from about January 20th throughout February 18th, again because it is in the middle of the season.
The mutable sign of the winter season is water sign Pisces, which ranges from February 19th throughout March 20th.
23. The sequence of the seasons are in order:

1. Spring
2. Summer
3. Autumn
4. Winter

It is therefore imperative as per biblical substantiation as well, that the beginning of the year has to be at the beginning of spring.
24. Should we proceed in accordance with our typical new year which commences at the first of January, we will be beginning our new year well into the winter season rather than Spring, which commences on the 22nd of March. It is of no surprise that the Chinese, Persians and Iranians have their new year set at the beginning of Spring in accordance with the season.
September meaning seven, October meaning eight, November meaning nine and December meaning ten….

Chapter 11: The Four Seasons Explained

....will all cause the months to fall in perfect alignment with the zodiacs in order for the beginning of the year to fall in perfect timing with the spring season.

25. *Seasonal Chart For Review*

Seasons	*Modules*	*Signs*	**Dates**	**Element**	**Core Char**
1. Spring	Cardinal	*Aries*	Mar 21-Apr 19	Fire	Choleric
	Fixed	*Taurus*	Apr 20-May 20	Earth	Melancholic
	Mutable	*Gemini*	May 21-Jun 20	Air	Sanguine
2. Summer	Cardinal	*Cancer*	Jun 21-Jul 22	Water	Phlegmatic
	Fixed	*Leo*	Jul 23-Aug 22	Fire	Choleric
	Mutable	*Virgo*	Aug 23-Sep 22	Earth	Melancholic
3. Autumn	Cardinal	*Libra*	Sep 23-Oct 22	Air	Sanguine
	Fixed	*Scorpio*	Oct 23-Nov 21	Water	Phlegmatic
	Mutable	*Sagitta*	Nov 22-Dec 21	Fire	Choleric
4. Winter	Cardinal	*Capric*	Dec 22-Jan 19	Earth	Melancholic
	Fixed	*Aquar*	Jan 20-Feb 18	Air	Sanguine
	Mutable	*Pisces*	Feb 19-Mar 20	Water	Phlegmatic

26. Upon concluding on the topic of the four seasons, may it be noted that the 4 seasons match the four corners of the earth, The four cardinal races (Red, Yellow, Black and White), the four cardinal directions, the four elements as well as the four core character types. The twelve zodiacs match the twelve months of the year, the twelve sub races that flow out of the four cardinal races as well as the 12 sub directions that flow out of the four basic ones.

Chapter 12:
The significance of one's day of birth

01. As per Galatians 4:4-6 ..When the fullness of the time was come, God sent forth his son, made of a woman, made under the law, to redeem them that were under the law that we might receive the adoption of sons….
The birth of Yeshuah, Samson, Moses, Samuel and many other great men had to be specifically orchestrated because they had a leading role to play in life. When demands are high a particular type of person is required whereby the specifications or gifts of each person is allotted to them by their time of birth.
02. We know that people born under cardinal signs will tend to have a stronger willed character at getting things done and establishing new ideas by core or by their nature, although they may not be able to execute as the fixed persons. We also know that people born under fixed signs are by nature more prone to be consistent in what they do and do not particularly like changes but are reliable to keep things going and get things done.
03. We also know that mutable persons can be very adaptable and can adjust to circumstances and are very open to change. It is therefore very likely or possible that Samson may have been an Aries whereas Aries people are by nature more physically inclined by nature. This does not mean that one would not find a Libra stronger or more physically endowed than an Aries, it just means that there's an underlying capacity that can contribute to the task with less effort.
04. It was also mentioned earlier in this book as to why there are exactly "four" gospels in the bible; There are "four" character types; namely Choleric, Phlegmatic, Sanguine and Melancholic.
Because each apostle was one of the four character types, telling the same story in their version would be ideal for the different types of characters found in people to be understood.

Chapter 12:
The significance of one's day of birth

05. The four gospels of the bible that tell the same story are Mathew, Mark, Luke and John. Also note that just as there are 12 zodiac signs, twelve months of the year, twelve sons of Jacob, twelve tribes of the earth; there were also twelve apostles. This genius structure makes it possible for the different types of people needed on earth to ensure that the right person is doing the appropriate thing according to his/her appropriate gifts. So yes our various talents and gifts are allotted to us based on our time of birth.

06. Mathew seemed to be a very detailed person and may have been a melancholic earth sign whereas Mark may have been a Phlegmatic water sign. This explains why he wrote the shortest book of the gospels, straight to the point. Luke may have been a choleric fire sign, whereas John may have been a sanguine air sign, as he was the only one to approach the capture of Christ from an optimistic perspective, clarifying that Christ wasn't captured helplessly whereas He pushed down 30 soldiers with his energy to ensure his disciples go free. (John 18:5-8)

07. Melancholic persons are known to be detailed, focused and grounded; they represent the earth signs. Phlegmatic persons are known to be laid back and inspirational; they do not care for leadership positions, but prefer to confirmedly know what they have to do, and do it. They are usually water signs who would like their own time to follow their hobby's in a spiritual and motivational manner.

08. Choleric people are the fire signed, serious, no nonsense persons who can become very angry if things aren't done the way they should be whereas Sanguine persons are the air signed optimistics who see the good in everything and can be fun loving "happy go lucky" people who detest fighting and controversy and would go to extremes to keep the peace.

Chapter 12:
The significance of one's day of birth

09. It is quite likely each disciple was a particular one of the twelve zodiacs; whereby Mathew, Mark, Luke and John were the four cardinals of the twelve signs. This also explains why John, who was one of the four cardinals, wrote the gospel and went on to do some serious prophetic writings in the book of revelation; a typical air sign who was very deep and could be used to pen the future in a prophetic and inspirational manner.
10. Just as there are four cardinal signs, which are four of the twelve zodiac signs; planet earth is also divided into twelve tribes, which are really twelve different cultures. It is for this reason Bible talks about the "four" corners of the earth in Revelation 7:1 as well as twelve tribes of the earth in Mathew 24:30 and specified as the twelve tribes of modern Israel in Revelation 21:12-14
11. Apparently in the old testament, the entire world at that time was divided into 12 different cultures. Each culture was deliberately explained as to what would befall them in the future as per Genesis 49. Reuben's descents were to be excellencies of power, Simeon and Levi instruments of cruelty, Judah was a lion's whelp, Zebulun's people are the sea people, Issachar's became servantile and Dan's became judges.
12. Gad's people will be over comers, Asher will yield royal dainties, Naphtali gives goodly words, Joseph a fruitful bough and Benjamin a ravin wolf.
It seems these tribes were the core that populated the world in that era, of which other nations came out of.
In the era of Christ's return, upon referring to the twelve tribes, there is one difference in that the 5th tribe which is of Dan is replaced by Manasseh.
13. Isn't it quite logical that we need the basic four types of people for the world to function competently? The four core characters are vital for the flow of the tide. Let us make a review of the following: ...

Chapter 12:
The significance of one's day of birth

....The Air signs are the Sanguine people who establish that things happen. The Fire signs, who are the Choleric people, establish the structure of the standard for things to happen.

14. The Earth signs are the Melancholic people who sustain the longevity of what has to continue to happen, whereas the Water Elements represent the Phlegmatic people who have the power to execute the procedures so as to make things happen. None of the four alone can be successful without the other. They all need each other and are all part of the puzzle that has to fit together

15. Each element fits into a certain area that has its contributing factor to their particular field. To give more clarity; air signs e.g. are ideal Judges, lawyers, business conglomerate directors, professors, spokes persons and ideal positions that are not particularly hands on. Earth elements are more prone to hands on jobs as they like to be involved in whatever is going on. Fire signs have to greatest capacity for more physical whereas Water signs are ideal for executive work.

16. Water signs who are often more spiritually inclined, can go into a spiritual zone whilst doing their routine work. They are in fact very spiritually connected and usually see into the spirit realm to an extreme that most of the other zodiacs do not, just as water is very emotional and responds to its surrounding; water signs are very intuitive and spiritual with a strong imaginative way of thinking that can flow into a variety of directions.

17. We must remember however that within every element there are three modules; the cardinal, the fixed and the mutable. The cardinal born persons are the initiators of their area of expertise that they were born into. The fixed born persons are the consistent persons of their area of expertise they were born into, whereas the mutable persons are the adaptive persons of their field of ....

Chapter 12: The significance of one's day of birth

....expertise that they were born into.

18. We revert to chapter 6 to the four core characters to recall that each element falls under one of the four chore characters; Sanguine, Melancholic, Phlegmatic and Choleric. Now each core character can also depict a section of one of the four fields that each element fits into.
E.g. 1. The none tangible fields 2. The high energy demanding fields 3. The physical demanding fields and 4. the executive jobs/fields.

19. Lets rephrase the same four as the mental, stressful, hands on and executive work jobs.
Air is not tangible so its more mental, air people are usually more analytic and mental people with great thoughts. Lawyers and judges who ideally weigh emotions and thoughts . Working in a mental institution or a residential facility for children between ages of 8 to 13 can be a job that mostly a high energy choleric fire sign may be able to handle.

20. This same choleric person may not have the capacity to be a security guard and do the routine work of opening and closing a gate for residents of a residential community. It would be much easier for a phlegmatic water sign to handle such a job. I'm in no way saying it doesn't or cannot happen, I'm saying which core character would handle which job with the least effort. This in no way implies that any particular zodiac sign or element cannot do the task of another; it rather depicts what comes easier.

21. The same phlegmatic person may work as a medical doctor but can't wait for 5 pm to go water skiing each day after work whilst a choleric sign may be seen late at nights, working to ensure that all procedures and administrations are up to par. When initiators work hard on setting up the structure, the fixed sign work hard on executing and the mutable come up with ideas to change things for adaptability, everything then flows harmoniously.

Chapter 12:
The significance of one's day of birth

22. There are 4 ways of being born cardinal; The various means of being born cardinal are as follows:

- The Month in which one was born
- The "day" on which one was born
- The numerology accumulation of when one was born
- The combination of more than one of the above

We will now delve into the various means of cardinality and discover why many people had the capacity to initiate certain trends in life.

23. The months of cardinality are most prominent; we first must disregard what we know as the typical months of the year and revert to the concept that the beginning of a year is at the beginning of Spring. This alignment is already in alignment with the zodiacs as per our chart below. Only then will it make sense that September is 7, October is 8, November is 9 and December means decimal is 10.

Seasons	*Months*	Dates	*Modules*	Elem.	Core Char
1. Spring	***1 Aries***	**Mar 21-Apr 19**	**Cardinal**	Fire	Choleric
	2 Taurus	Apr 20-May 20	Fixed	Earth	Melancholic
	3 Gemini	May 21-Jun 20	Mutable	Air	Sanguine
2. Summer	***4 Cancer***	**Jun 21-Jul 22**	**Cardinal**	Water	Phlegmatic
	5 Leo	Jul 23-Aug 22	Fixed	Fire	Choleric
	6 Virgo	Aug 23-Sep 22	Mutable	Earth	Melancholic
3. Autumn	***7 Libra***	**Sep 23-Oct 22**	**Cardinal**	Air	Sanguine
	8 Scorpio	Oct 23-Nov 21	Fixed	Water	Phlegmatic
	9 Sagittarius	Nov 22-Dec 21	Mutable	Fire	Choleric
4. Winter	***10 Capricorn***	**Dec 22-Jan 19**	**Cardinal**	Earth	Melancholic
	11 Aquarius	Jan 20-Feb 18	Fixed	Air	Sanguine
	12 Pisces	Feb 19-Mar 20	Mutable	Water	Phlegmatic

Chapter 12:
The significance of one's day of birth

24. To summarize the cardinality of the month as per the stipulated chart on prior page; The first most prominent source of being cardinal would be based on birth in the beginning of one of the four seasons: I Aries (beginning of Spring), II Cancer (Beginning of Summer, III Libra (The beginning of Autumn) or IV Capricorn the beginning of Winter. The secondary source of being Cardinal would be being born on a certain day:

25. This second source of being cardinal is by being born on a certain "day of the week". Just as the sun is at its highest peak at midday, a week is at its highest peak on a Wednesday. Wednesday is also called "hump day" whereas it is in fact the exact middle of a work week or a general week as per stipulation below:

- 1.Monday - 2.Tuesday - **3.Wednesday** - 4.Thursday - 5.Friday
- 1.Sunday - 2.Monday - 3.Tuesday - **4.Wednesday** - 5.Thursday - 6.Friday - 7.Saturday

26. So as stipulated above, whether by a 5 day work week or a regular 7 day week, Wednesdays are always in the exact middle of a week just as the sun is in the middle of the sky at noon as per each time zone. To know if someone is born on a Wednesday, one would have to check their exact date of birth and see what day of the week the date of birth fell on. E.g. if Joe was born on February 25th in the year of 1981, Joe would have been born on a Wednesday. So although Joe wasn't born In a cardinal month, Joe will still be Cardinal and exhibit leadership qualities.

27. It is therefore possible to use a calendar or check online to assess what day of the week various persons were born on in order to determine their cardinality by means of day of the week. We will therefore see certain people who were not born on a cardinal date, but were born on a cardinal day and therefore function...

Chapter 12:
The significance of one's day of birth

...in a cardinal manner. I have encountered many great leaders and initiators who were not born on a Cardinal date. However when I learnt about the cardinal day of birth (Wednesdays), my eyes opened to see that it was explainable.

28. We now venture into the third manner by which a person can be cardinal: This is by numerology or life path number. This is a theory by which a person's date, month and year of birth is added up. After adding the outcome of the number it can be determined in this manner if the numerical additional value totals particular numbers. The numerical value of the numbers 1,4 & 8 are cardinal numbers and 11,22 or 33 are called master numbers: All would deem an individual to be cardinal as well.

29. I will first explain the meaning of the numbers additions, after which I will then illustrate the manner in which the additions and numerical values are applied. Those who have Life Path Number 1 are known to be **courageous leaders**. They tend not to get influenced by others and like to be the only ones to control their freedom and hold onto it. They are self-dependent and do not rely on others.

30. As per Google If you're a life path 2, it means you're motivated by community, harmony, and relationships. Life path 2s are peacekeepers who aim to achieve balance, specifically when it comes to their relationships. They're sensitive empaths, so they can pick up the emotions of others, and they're generally reserved and kindhearted. Let's now move on the life path number three.

31. As per Google; People with a Life Path Number of 3 are creative spirits driven by their infinite imagination. They're all about fun and living their life to its fullest while spreading joy to others.

Chapter 12: The significance of one's day of birth

...Life Path Number 3's can be disorganized at times and have trouble committing to one hobby or career path People with a Life Path Number of 3 are creative spirits driven by their infinite imagination. They're all about fun and living their life to its fullest while spreading joy to others. Life Path Number 3's can be disorganized at times and have trouble committing to one hobby or career path

32. As per Google's meaning of four in numerology. The Life Path Number 4 is associated with people who are practical, sensible, pragmatic and rational by nature. They are quite methodical and well ordered apart from being efficient in their essence. It means they have a rational thought process while making any decision in life. Life path four are energetic, knowledgeable, clever and confident with **leadership skills.** They are good with keeping secrets, love, creativity and have a sharp memory. Weaknesses are that they can be rebellious and overconfident at times leading to negative traits.

33. As per Google...Life Path Number 5 are a multi-talented individuals who crave freedom, adventure, and excitement, and your roles in life (you will have at least two or three careers!) need to deliver that in order to capture your attention.

34. As per Google: The Life Path Number 6 is associated with a lot of love, affection, care, and humility. You are someone who likes to serve humanity for a more significant cause. You have a lot of empathy towards the ones who are weak and are suffering. It gives you immense joy to help people.

35. As per Google: Someone with life path number 7 is the logical mystic, the spiritual analyst, the lonely humanitarian, the truth-seeker. Sevens are super smart, curious, and eager to create progressive resolutions to worldly problems. They will use any form of knowledge or insight to reach their goals .

Chapter 12:
The significance of one's day of birth

36. As per Google; In Numerology, people with the Life Path Number 8 are usually associated with being natural and prolific leaders. They have excellent management skills and are always up to achieving something great, especially when involved in financial or business matters.
39. As per Google; People with a life path number 9 have the ability to let go and embrace others with different life path numbers. They are flexible and open-minded, with a strong sense of creativity. In terms of professional life, number 9 individuals may excel in technology, medicine, construction, or defense jobs.
40. As per Google: Life Path Number 10 can be reduced to the single digit 1, because 1 + 0 = 1.
As per Google: There are three master numbers: **11, 22, and 33**. A master number holds special significance because it offers double the power of the number it doubles from. According to the ethics of numerology, master numbers are never reduced back to a sum vibration of 1 through 9 .
41. Now as we see the master numbers, are only doubles of 1,2 and 3. The numbers 4,5,6,7,8 and 9 are not doubled to acquire master numbers. Some of the numbers that are not double or master numbers are already cardinal within themselves. E.g. the single numbers 1, 4 and 8 are cardinal as they all have leadership potential (cardinal). A 22 or 33 will not be as powerful in a master number as the number 11 whereas 1 is already cardinal.
42. The 22 master number is a double of the number 2, but the number 2 is not cardinal within itself. The number 1 is deemed cardinal and has leadership skill, an 11 therefore is almost double cardinal in being a master nr. of the number 1. It is now time to decipher how to calculate life path numbers in the proper manner. Joe who was born on Feb 25th 1981 is calculated in this manner.
25 02 1981 (2+5+2+1+9+8+1=28 / 2+8=10 / 1+0=**1).**

Chapter 12:
The significance of one's day of birth

43. Lets see how many cardinality Joe has:

- A. Joe was born on February 25th and is therefore a Pisces and is a mutable water sign. Joe is not a cardinal zodiac sign by date of birth.
- B. Joe's day of birth stemming from his year and day; Joe was born on a Wednesday which is a Cardinal day; Joe is therefore cardinal by "day".
- C. Joe's life path number is '1" as was calculated on previous page; as 1 has leadership skills; Joe is therefore cardinal by life path number

44. Joe is therefore double cardinal and will function on an extreme high capacity that will surpass his educational or social status as Joe is double cardinal. My queen who is in reality a triple cardinal, was born on a Wednesday, is cardinal earth plus an 11 in her life path master number; This will explain why she had the drive to reach the highest in her career with higher grades than the rest of the class in addition to being the youngest graduate of the class. It also explains the capacity to handle multiple projects that may be deemed tedious for one person.

45. People with cardinal status are usually sent into the world to change, fix or do something. Such examples can be seen in the likes of Martin Luther King Jr. Martin Luther King Jr was born a cardinal earth sign on January 15th 1929 and was cardinal by date of birth. He was also born on a Tuesday, which is close to a Wednesday. If his time of birth was Tuesday after sunset, he would've been born on a Wednesday, which is a cardinal day; so its possible his day of birth was cardinal, if not, it was close to a cardinal Wednesday.

46. The life path number of Martin Luther King Jr. was as follows: 15 01 1929 = 1+5+0+1+1+9+2+9 = 28 / 2+8=**1** which is a cardinal life path number. Martin Luther King Jr. had a job to liberate the extremity of racism from the world, and he did just that.

Chapter 12: The significance of one's day of birth

47. The beginning of a day begins when the sun sets and not at midnight. The sundial which actually reveals what time it is based on the shadow of the sun, is what really determines the time of day. For stability in time, man has established a day to begin at midnight, which is actually incorrect. As per Genesis 1:5 [5]**And God called the light Day, and the darkness he called Night. And the evening and the morning were the first day.**

48. Because evening begins at sunset, it is used to depict the entire night time. Morning which begins at sunrise depicts the entire day time. Evening and morning therefore means the entire night time and the entire daytime completes a day. Please note that the night time of a day is the first part of a day whereas the day time depicts the second part of a day. For this reason we deem the evening of December 24th Christmas "eve" night and not the night of December 25th.

49. There are over 500 Sabbath keeping religions that all keep God's weekly Sabbaths; this includes real Rastafarians. Sabbath commences at sunset on Friday evening for these people and ends at sunset on Saturday. If someone is therefore deemed to be born on a Tuesday, when they were born on Tuesday after sunset, they then would've in reality have been born on a Wednesday rather than Tuesday. We then have to confirm carefully the time of birth when someone is said to have been born in the evening rather than the daytime.

50. It is for this reason that we reconsider the time of birth for those who were said to be born on a Tuesday. Howbeit being born a day before or after will most likely have an effect on one's cardinality nonetheless. Let us continue to review the life of another cardinal person; Mahatma Gandhi was born a Cardinal air sign on October 2nd 1869. He was an Indian lawyer and activist who lead a none violent resistance campaign against the British and

Chapter 12:
The significance of one's day of birth

....India released from under the rule of Great Britain.

51. Cardinal Air sign Libra is known to be the sign that produces the most billionaires in the world; There's a list that consists of the likes of … Giovanni Ferrero, Ralph Lauren, Ken Griffin, Serena Williams, Alice Walton of Wal-Mart, Bruce Springsteen and Simon Cowell of American Idol amongst others. There are many other wealthy cardinals who refuse to accept exposure or sometimes conceal their wealth in holding companies.

53. Jeremiah 1:5 Before I formed thee in the belly I knew thee; and before thou camest forth out of the womb I sanctified thee, and I ordained thee a prophet unto the nations.

The Bible text above gives substantiation to the fact that we are all born to fulfill a particular purpose in life even prior to being born. No birth is an accident or a coincidence; no one is an accident.

54. Cardinal people were born to initiate, Fixed powerhouses were born to execute and Mutable people were born to initiate adaptation for change and growth. This concept of the three different types of people are again a symbolic number of completion. Some of us may notice that passing on also often comes in three's. The concept of the Trinity comes in a group of three. In Baptism; the concept whereby a person can be reborn as a citizen of heaven has a threefold vow.

55. As per Mathew 28:19 we are to baptize people in the name of 1.The Father 2.The Son and 3.The Holy Spirit. Cardinal, Fixed and Mutable are a replica of the completeness of what we know as the trinity. The Father is the head and is the cardinal force of the Godhead..the leader; this is acknowledged by his son Yeshuah (John 14:28 / John 5:19). Yeshuah even went as far as to acknowledge that He didn't come to earth on His own, that His Father Sent Him (John 8:42).

Chapter 12:
The significance of one's day of birth

<u>**56.**</u> Pay keen attention to the exact words uttered by Yeshuah Himself, whereby He himself is saying with His own words from His own mouth that His Father <u>is greater / superior to Him.</u> Also be reminded that in His own words, He confirmed that it wasn't His idea to come to save planet earth, but His Father (The leader of the Godhead) sent Him. 1st Corinthians 8:6 is hereby reconfirming that there is in actuality only "1" GOD (The Father) and that "everything" and "everyone" (Including Yeshuah) came from Him and 1 Lord Yeshuah The Christ and we by Him.
<u>**57.**</u> The Cardinal Father, the Leader, sent His Son to create the earth, then to save it (John 3:16). The Son is who executed the creation of the world and for this reason is called "lord" of creation or Lord of the earth. The Son represents fixed signs who execute the ideas of the Cardinal (s). Lord comes from the word landlord. Landlord means owner of the property; the one from whom we rent the building or apartment. So a Lord is the owner of property. Yeshuah is called Lord of creation because it was He who created the planet...the executioner of the Father's will. He is co-owner because He is the Son of the Father.
<u>**58.**</u> We can say that the Father is the ultimate owner, the Son is co-owner, but what or who is the Holy Spirit also known as The Holy Ghost, who was deemed the mutable force of the Godhead? To understand who or what the Holy Spirit or Holy Ghost is, we must first understand what the word spirit and ghost means. In John 13:21-22 it says Yeshuah was troubled in His spirit; This meant his "mind" or thoughts were disturbed. In Isaiah 63:10 it is expressed that the people "vexed" God's Holy Spirit; This means that they annoyed Him.
<u>**59.**</u> When traditionally it is said that one saw or felt the presence of a spirit or ghost, it usually means that they felt the conscious presence of usually a deceased person.

Chapter 12:
The significance of one's day of birth

60. It means the conscious presence of a person without their body. In one of Ellen White's books it is mentioned that Ellen's spirit (consciousness) left her body and went to another world and met Enoch, whom she asked if he lives there, Enoch replied that he was just visiting. In the meantime Ellen's body was left holding a rather heavy book in her hand whilst her spirit was in another world. Does this mean that there are two Ellen's ? No it doesn't.
61. Story continues that Ellen was so impressed with how beautiful that other world was and how dark and unappealing the world that she came from was, that she didn't want to return. She had to be coaxed and be explained why she had to return.
Point is: God's Spirit or Ghost simply means His presence in consciousness; not a third person but "His" person; His thoughts. Our thoughts are what truly defines who we are.
62. For more clarification on this topic; Our central nervous system which is known as our penal gland is what allows our bodies to experience the feeling of touch, even sexual arousal. When someone touches our hands or legs, it is not the actual hand or leg that feels the touch, it is our nervous system that is connected to that secret place in our brain that the signal goes to that lets us feel the touch.
63. A medical doctor can deaden e.g. the nervous system in a leg and literally take an ax and cut off that leg whilst we watch and we wouldn't feel anything because no signal went to the central nervous system in the brain. That central nervous system in the brain is what connects our "spirit" to our bodies; So when someone dies their "spirit" or "ghost" is released from the body; hence the term in James; the "body" without the spirit is dead (James 2:26)
64. There is so much more information to be released regarding spirit, but we will leave the more in depth infor….

Chapter 12:
The significance of one's day of birth

….-mation for our next book to come, which will be named "Who GOD really is". Our actions are usually the result of our thoughts (our spirit). E.g. there's a pen laying across the table, our mind processes the thought to reach it to write with. After the thought processed we reach for that pen or ask someone to reach it for us.

65. In Genesis 1: 1-3 It says God created the heavens and the earth; It confirms that there was darkness and that water was covering everywhere. Note how prior to commanding light to appear that The Spirit (His consciousness/thoughts) moved over the surface of the waters prior to commanding light to appear, in order to commence or continue with the recreation of planet earth.

66. Now that I think we've provided sufficient evidence to confirm what spirit/ghost means, we can now continue with the concept whereby the Holy Spirit/Ghost is deemed the comparable mutable force of The Godhead. We now understand why The Father is Cardinal; He's the Initiator. We understand why The Son Yeshuah is the Fixed sign; He's the executioner; the one who actually created the our world. Now let us indulge in the concept of the Holy Spirit being the mutable force.

67. Mutable as we recall from chapter 10 means to bring change or adaptability. We explained how people born at the beginning of a season are cardinal, those born in the middle of any season are called fixed and those born at the end or change of any season are called mutable people. Mutable people changes things or adapts to change; they influence change.

The Holy Spirit does just that, it changes our nature and gives us power to "adapt" to the changes/challenges we encounter in life.

68. In John 20:22 Yeshuah gave the disciples a higher percentage of the Holy Spirit in order to have more power to adapt to do greater things.

Chapter 12: The significance of one's day of birth

....It is therefore from that perspective we may again summarize the same sequence of the Godhead as God being Cardinal, Yeshuah Fixed and the Holy Spirit Mutable Psalms 139:13-15 is saying that everyone was wonderfully made and serves a purpose to fit into a master plan.

69. The various character types and the gifts that we all possess is a compilation of our time of birth as well as the numerical value of our birth. No one is a coincidence and no one is useless. Circumstances may cause someone to be living on the street in poverty but we are our brother's keeper, each one of us should embark on the mission to help our fellowmen aspire to what they were meant to be. There is potential in everyone that needs to be released, there is a purpose for their lives that needs to fit into the flow of life.

70. When a student is in high school, and it is time to chose which subjects he or she should keep, it is a good start to focus on what he or she is already good at. It is also a guide as to what their role in life is destined to be. There's a saying that goes: Find a job doing what you love to do and you will never have to work a day in your life. If we look closely at our strengths and weaknesses we will see clearly that they are aligned with our time of birth, day of birth, numerical value of our birth in collaboration with the combination of all.

71. What we need to take into consideration however, is the following; If a person is e.g. a cardinal air sign, whose temperament should be Sanguine, but their numerical value of date of birth is e.g. a "2", we may see traits of choleric or phlegmatic in their character. One may then state that the time of birth as a cardinal air sign does not match up with what he or she aught to be, but this will be due to the combining factors of the other cardinal aspects that all have an affect on the person. It is therefore imperative or advisable that we consider all the factors.

Chapter 12:
The significance of one's day of birth

72. Another great example is; if a person is a cardinal earth sign and based on their zodiac they would be more inclined to be melancholic; it means that they would by nature prefer to control things from behind the scenes and would prefer not to be the center of attention. However if their numerical value of their date of birth is a cardinal "11" e.g., this person would have the capacity to be upfront and take the bull by the horns.
73. The combination of what we are is the deciding factor of our talents, which makes provision for God to provide us our gifts which will empower us to fulfill the purpose for our lives. When one was designated for a divine purpose, they usually will fulfill it, no matter what decisions they make in life. A prime example of this is the story of Simon in Judges chapters 13 and 14. Samson was born for the role of defeating the Philistines who had God's people enslaved.
74. Although Samson went against the rules and married a woman from the enemy instead of his own, he still got into contentions with the philistines and ended up fighting against them. Circumstances or destiny still lead him to fight against them despite the forbidden intermarriage. He gave out the secret to his strength whereby he was captured. Although he was in captivity and bound in chains, he asked for the power, received it and "still" destroyed all the philistines at his premature death.
75. There are times when great people fulfill their mission and die shortly after. Moses died before the Israelites got to the promised land. Samson died when he killed the Philistines. Martin Luther King Jr. after leaving his trend. Myles Munroe died after his kingdom message. The apostle Peter as well as other disciples died after their mission was accomplished. There is no defeat in death, victory is in doing what is right; Moses, Samson, John the Baptist all went to a better place better than here.

Chapter 12: The significance of one's day of birth

76. What is important is that we find the purpose for which we were born and fulfill it; Everyone has it. People like Peter, Moses, Martin and many others may've wanted to leave to go to a better place. John the revelator didn't have that temperament. God doesn't give us more than we can bare, which is why John was exiled instead of persecuted. The date of birth, day of birth, numerical value of birth and combination thereof gives a good guideline to your purpose for being here; follow the signs and find it.
77. I encourage you to discover who you really are and fulfill the role in life that was laid out for you even before you were conceived in your mother's womb. We are all part of a master plan. We can only do this if we unite as a force of one and utilize the powers that were allotted to us. Cartoon character captain planet is a great illustration of the power of the elements united, remember each of us represent an element that can become indestructible when united.
78. In closing I wish to remind our youth to pay attention to the subjects in school that they master effortlessly and enjoy doing. This is a key factor and a great guideline to following the path to your destiny. Find your talents and they will open the doors to receive your gifts. When one's talents and gifts are united as a force of one is when one will know their role and purpose in life. If rephrased I can say when one's career and spiritual destiny become united is when one reaches the path of enlightenment in knowing their purpose in life. Follow the signs and discover who you are and then be the best version of the man or woman you were meant to be !
79. A combination chart of the philosophical flow is displayed on the following page. Should there be any corrections to be made, we will ensure to update in or subsequent book. It however gives some perspective to the philosophical application of life.

Chapter 12:
The significance of one's day of birth

Compilation Chart

Card Dir	*Race*	*Seasons*	*Months*	Dates	*Modules*	Elem.	Core	Vocals	Nume
East	**Yellow**	**I. Spring**	***1 Aries***	**Mar 21-Apr 19**	**Cardinal**	Fire	Choleric	Tenor	1.
			2 Taurus	Apr 20-May 20	Fixed	Earth	Melancholic	Bass	
			3 Gemini	May 21-Jun 20	Mutable	Air	Sanguine	Lead	
South	**Black**	**II. Summer**	***4 Cancer***	**Jun 21-Jul 22**	**Cardinal**	Water	Phlegmatic	Baritone	4.
			5 Leo	Jul 23-Aug 22	Fixed	Fire	Choleric	*Tenor*	
			6 Virgo	Aug 23-Sep 22	Mutable	Earth	Melancholic	*Bass*	
West	**Red**	**III. Autumn**	***7 Libra***	**Sep 23-Oct 22**	**Cardinal**	Air	Sanguine	*Lead*	7.
			8 Scorpio	Oct 23-Nov 21	Fixed	Water	Phlegmatic	*Baritone*	
			9 Sagittarius	Nov 22-Dec 21	Mutable	Fire	Choleric	*Tenor*	
North	**White**	**IV. Winter**	***10 Capricorn***	**Dec 22-Jan 19**	**Cardinal**	Earth	Melancholic	*Bass*	10.
			11 Aquarius	Jan 20-Feb 18	Fixed	Air	Sanguine	*Lead*	
			12 Pisces	Feb 19-Mar 20	Mutable	Water	Phlegmatic	*Baritone*	

...

NOTES

NOTES

Made in the USA
Columbia, SC
03 April 2025

56090934R00046